ABOUT THE AUTHOR

Moustafa Gadalla was born in Cairo, Egypt in 1944. He graduated from Cairo University with a Bachelor of Science degree in civil engineering in 1967. He immigrated to the U.S.A. in 1971 and continued to practice engineering as a licensed professional engineer and land surveyor. He is an independent Egyptologist who spent most of his adult life studying, and researching scores of books about Egyptology, mythology, religions, the Bible, languages, etc.

He is the author of six internationally-acclaimed books about ancient Egypt. He is the chairman of the Tehuti Research Foundation, an international, U.S.-based, non-profit organization, dedicated to ancient Egypt

D1617248

OTHER BOOKS BY T.

Historical Deception
The Untold Story of Ancient Egypt (2nd Ed.)
ISBN: 0-9652509-2-X (pbk.), 352 pages, US$19.95

Egyptian Cosmology: The Absolute Harmony
ISBN: 0-9652509-1-1 (pbk.), 160 pages, US$9.95

Pyramid Handbook
ISBN: 0-9652509-4-6 (pbk.), 192 pages, US$11.95

Exiled Egyptians: The Heart of Africa
ISBN: 0-9652509-6-2 (pbk.), 352 pages, US$19.95

Egypt: A Practical Guide
ISBN: 0-9652509-3-0 (pbk.), 256 pages, US$8.50

Tut-Ankh-Amen: The Living Image of the Lord
ISBN: 0-9652509-9-7 (pbk.), 144 pages, US$9.50

Acknowledgement

Special thanks to Jason Just, my enlightened musician friend from New Zealand, for his assistance and contribution to the musical aspect of this book.

Book Cover Artwork by K&D Design, North East, PA, USA

Egyptian Harmony

The *Visual* Music

Moustafa Gadalla

Maa Kheru (True of Voice)

Tehuti Research Foundation
International Head Office: Greensboro, NC, U.S.A.

Egyptian Harmony: The Visual Music

by MOUSTAFA GADALLA

Published by:

Tehuti Research Foundation
P.O. Box 39406
Greensboro, NC   27438-9406, U.S.A.

Publisher's Cataloging-in-Publication
(Provided by Quality Books, Inc.)

Gadalla, Moustafa, 1944-
    Egyptian harmony : the visual music / Moustafa Gadalla (Maa Kheru). -- 1st ed.
    p. cm.
    Includes bibliographical references and index.
    Includes index.
    LCCN: 00-90717
    ISBN: 0-9652509-8-9

    1. Aesthetics, Egyptian. 2. Harmony (Aesthetics) 3. Architecture--Egypt--Aesthetics.
    4. Proportion (Art) 5. Egypt--Antiquities.
    6. Egypt--Civilization--To 332 B.C. I. Title.

BH221.E2G26 2000   701.17'0932
                    QBI00-558

Manufactured in the United States of America
Published 2000

Table of Contents

Preface

Herodotus, the father of history and a native Greek, stated in 500 BCE:

"Now, let me talk more of Egypt for it has a lot of admirable things and what one sees there is superior to any other country."

The superior ancient Egyptian monuments are the physical manifestation of their superior cosmic knowledge, for, as stated in Asleptus III *(25)* of *Hermetic Texts:*

"...in Egypt all the operations of the powers which rule and work in heaven have been transferred to earth below...it should rather be said that the whole cosmos dwells in [Egypt] as in its sanctuary..."

Therefore, we must forego viewing the ancient Egyptian monuments as an interplay of forms against a vague historical, archeological presentation. Instead, we must try to see it as the dwelling place of the cosmos, as the relationship between form and function.

Johann Wolfgang von Goethe (1749-1832) described architecture as "frozen music". In ancient Egypt, architecture was animated visual music — definitely not frozen. Egyptian architecture and art followed the principles of harmonic dynamic design that equally applies to sound and form.

Sound and form are two sides of the same coin, and their relationship is equated to the metaphysical and physical aspects of the universe.

The physical manifestation of the universe is a masterpiece of order, harmony, and beauty. The architecture of bodily existence is determined by an invisible, immaterial world of pure form and geometry.

The ancient Egyptians, who were/are known as doers (builders), put their knowledge and wisdom into animated, energetic, productive works.

With a pure heart and a pure mind, let us enjoy the beauty and power of the universe from the Temple of the Cosmos — Egypt.

Moustafa Gadalla
July, 2000

Standards and Terminology

1 - The ancient Egyptian word **neter**, and its feminine form **netert**, have been wrongly, and possibly intentionally, translated to *god* and *goddess*, by almost all academicians. **Neteru** (plural of **neter/netert**) are the divine principles and functions that operate the universe. They are all aspects and functions of the One Supreme God.

2 - When referring to the names of cities, Pharaohs, **neteru** (gods/goddesses), etc., if the commonly used Greek name is different than the true Egyptian name, we will show the correct Egyptian name followed by the common (but arbitrary) Greek rendering between parentheses.

3 - To make it easier for the reader, we will give a "value" to a ratio/proportion between two integer numbers, even though it is not. We will also write angle measurements (in degrees, etc.) to make it easier for "modern education", even though it is inferior to the principles of *sacred geometry*.

4 - Because of the importance of the Egyptian cord of 12 equal intervals with 13 knots, we divided the book into 13 (but unequal) knots instead of chapters.

5 - Throughout this book, the fonting of quotations varies depending on the source of quotation. There are generally two types of fonting:

Δ *This font is used to refer to ancient Egyptian sources.*

Δ *This font is to refer to quotes from other sources.*

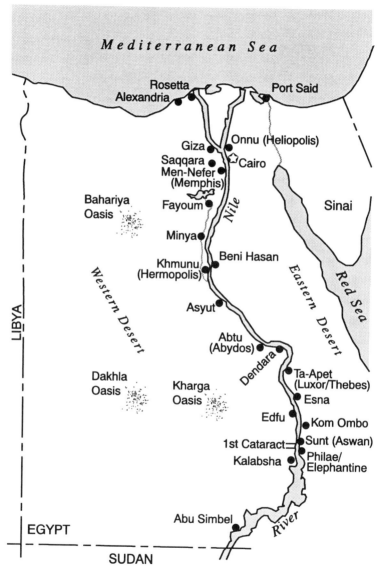

Egypt (Present-Day)

𝒦not 1

For Your Eyes/Ears Only

Harmony Defined

The origin of the English word *harmony* is the Greek word, *harmos*, which means *to join*. By *harmony*, we generally mean a fitting, orderly, and pleasant joining of diversities, which in themselves may harbor many contrasts.

In ancient Egypt, Ra is described in The Litany of Ra as

The One Joined [harmoniously] Together.

Harmony applies to both sound (music) and form (architecture). The use of musically derived harmonies in architecture was held to be expressive of the Divine Harmony engendered at the act of creation by the Word (sound) — in modern terms, the Big Bang that began the Universe.

The intimate relationship in ancient Egypt between harmony in music and architecture is reflected in their language where the word for a building is the same as the word for a stanza. The Arabic language follows the same thinking where the word pronounced as *bait* means both a house and a stanza.

The hieroglyphs above the doorway of the house shown here read: **"the good/beautiful abode"** —

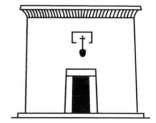

the ultimate visual music.

The design of ancient Egyptian architecture was based on proportion. Musical harmonies are likewise based on proportion. It has been said that music is in reality geometry translated into sound, for in music the same harmonies can be heard, which underlie architectural proportion.

The Masons claim that their rites, knowledge and traditions are rooted in Egypt, and there are many indications to support that. The famed Mozart was a Mason, just like his father and many notable people in his era. His music was the spirit of the past of the ancient Egyptian traditions. His crowning achievement was the Masonic Opera, where the power of masonry becomes the power of music by using Masonic symbols.

Kepler and the Egyptian Renaissance

Western academia tells us that Johannes Kepler (1571-1630) discovered the three planetary laws:

Law 1. The orbit of a planet/comet about the Sun is an ellipse with the sun's center of mass at one focus.

Law 2. A line joining a planet/comet and the Sun sweeps out equal areas in equal intervals of time.

Law 3. The squares of the periods of the planets are proportional to the cubes of their semi-major axes.

Yet none of these Western academicians tells us how Kepler arrived (out of thin air) at these conclusions. In truth, Kepler boasted in print, at the end of *Book V* of his series, *Harmony of the World*, that he <u>rediscovered the lost laws of Egypt</u>, as noted below:

"Now, eighteen months after the first light, three months after the true day, but a very few days after the pure Sun of that most wonderful study began to shine, nothing restrains me; <u>it is my pleasure to yield to the inspired frenzy, it is my pleasure to taunt mortal men with the candid acknowledgment that I am stealing the golden vessels of the Egyptians to build a tabernacle to my God from them, far, far away from the boundaries of Egypt.</u> If you forgive me, I shall rejoice; if you are enraged with me, I shall bear it. See, I cast the die, and I write the book. Whether it is to be read by the people of the present or of the future makes no difference: let it await its reader for a hundred years, if God Himself has stood ready for six thousand years for one to study him."

The jubilant Kepler did not state that he himself discovered anything. Rather it was all ancient Egyptian. His work on planetary laws and everything else followed the strict ancient Egyptian thinking that:

1) All creations (sound/form) must be defined within the perimeter of a circle.

   ☥ In ancient Egypt, it is Ra whose symbol is the circle that is the archetype of creation.

2) All proportions and measurements of figures can only be drawn or created using a straight line (not even a ruler) and a compass.

   ☥ All ancient Egyptian executed work shows that they adhered to these principles, known in the Western world as *sacred geometry*.

Kepler's insistence on following these lines bewildered his Western commentaries, who did not understand Kepler's reason for not "benefitting" from other Greek-attributed works (such as Plato, Pythagoras, and Euclid). Kepler was, by virtue of his work, a revivalist of ancient Egyptian achievements.

The Egyptian Sacred Cord

Temples and other buildings in ancient Egypt were laid out in a religious ceremony. This laying out was performed by very knowledgeable people who are known by the Greek name, *harpedonaptae.* The vain Greeks usually likened their "notable" people to the harpedonaptae, indicative of the latter's extensive knowledge.

The harpedonaptae are the people who strictly adhered to the principles of sacred geometry, as explained on the previous page (using only a straight line and a compass). Their cord was (and still is, in parts of present-day Egypt) a very special cord that consists of a 13-knotted rope with 12 equally-spaced distances of one Egyptian cubit (1.72' or 0.5236m).

The origin of the historic building layout was the setting out of the 3:4:5 triangle with the Egyptian rope, wound about three pegs so that it formed three sides measuring three, four, and five units, which provides a 90° angle between its 3 and 4 sides.

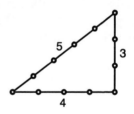

It was a relatively simple task to lay out rectangles and other more complex geometrical figures after establishing the 3:4:5 right-angle triangle.

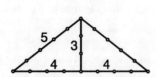
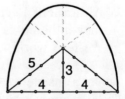

The Egyptian cord can be used as a compass to draw circular curves, as shown in the above right diagram.

Other shapes such as the 5:8 **Neb** (Golden) triangle or rectangle, as shown below, can also be established with the Egyptian cord. [More about the significance of these shapes later on in this book.]

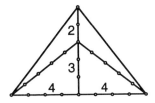 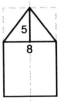

The cord is/was a measuring device. The term *measure* applies to music, metrology, time, etc. In essence, all these various applications of the term, *measure*, are similar.

The hieroglyphic symbol for **Ra**, the cosmic creative force, is the circle. When the cord is looped as a full circle, the archetype of creation, we find that the radius of this sacred circle equals 1.91 cubits. In converting this measurement of

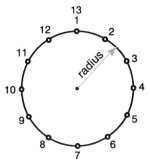

1.91 cubits of the radius into the metric system, we get 1 meter exactly (1.91 x 0.5236).

1 meter = 1/100,000[th] part of the quarter of the earth's meridian. In other words, this particular 13-knotted Egyptian rope, and the Egyptian unit of measurement known as a *cubit* are based on the measurement of the earth' circumference.

Throughout this book, you will find this cord to be the basic tool used to establish the sacred geometric shapes and their musical significance.

Egyptian Mystery Plays (Encyclopedia in Action)

To understand ancient Egypt, one must understand their mode of expression. Understanding them through Western paradigms is a lost cause.

The totality of the Egyptian civilization was built upon a complete and precise understanding of universal laws. This profound understanding manifested itself in a consistent, coherent and interrelated system, where art, science, philosophy and religion were intertwined, and were employed simultaneously in a single organic Unity.

The cosmological knowledge of ancient Egypt was expressed in a story form, which is a superior means for expressing both physical and metaphysical concepts. Any good writer or lecturer knows that stories are better than exposition for explaining the behavior of things, because the relationships of parts to each other, and to the whole, are better maintained by the mind.

The ancient Egyptians avoided abstracts. The Egyptian sagas transformed common factual nouns and adjectives (indicators of qualities) into proper but conceptual nouns. These were, in addition, personified so that they could be woven into narratives, like a sacred drama or mystery play, which can be easily digested.

Personification is based on their knowledge that man was made in the image of God, and as such, man represented the created image of all creation.

Plutarch's *Moralia, Vol V* explains some aspects of the Egyptian way:

The Egyptians simply give the name of Ausar [Osiris]
to the whole source and faculty creative of moisture,

believing this to be the cause of generation and the substance of life-producing seed; and the name of Set [Typhon in Greek] they give to all that is dry, fiery, and arid, in general, and antagonistic to moisture.

As the Egyptians regard the Nile as the effusion of Ausar [Osiris], so they hold and believe the earth to be the body of Auset [Isis], not all of it, but so much of it as the Nile covers, fertilizing it and uniting with it. From this union they make Heru [Horus] to be born. The all-conserving and fostering Hora, that is the seasonable tempering of the surrounding air, is Heru [Horus].

The insidious scheming and usurpation of Set [Typhon], then, is the power of drought, which gains control and dissipates the moisture which is the source of the Nile and of its rising.

Ausar (Water)   Auset (Earth)

Heru (Air)   Set (Fire)

The Egyptian Personification of the Four Elements of Solidity

We find the same characters/energies/powers in the legendary tale of **Ausar** (Osiris) and **Auset** (Isis), their son **Heru** (Horus), and the evil one, **Set** (Seth/Typhon). The relationship between the father, mother, and son are analogous to the right-angle triangle 3:4:5. [More details later in Knots 6 and 8.]

These well-crafted mystery plays are an intentionally chosen means for communicating knowledge. Meaning and the mystical experience are not tied to a literal interpretation of events. Nobody should dwell on the actors (characters), but on what they each represent. Once the inner meanings of the narratives have been revealed, they become marvels of simultaneous scientific and philosophical completeness and conciseness. The more they are studied, the richer they become. And, rooted in the narrative as it is, the part can never be mistaken for the whole, nor can its functional significance be forgotten or distorted.

•   •   •

The religious texts of Egypt reveal that the Egyptians believed in One God, who was self-produced, self-existent, immortal, invisible, eternal, omniscient, almighty, etc.

Ancient Egyptians avoided abstracts, and as such this One God was never represented and has no name. The closest thing to the term God in ancient Egypt is **Amen-Renef**, which means *He Whose Real Essence is Unknown*. In other words, they never called a name in vain.

One can only define "God" through the multitude of his attributes/qualities/powers/actions. This is the only logical way, because if we refer to, say, a person as Mr. X, it means nothing to us. However, once we know his attributes and qualities, we then begin to know him.

It is therefore that the functions and attributes of **Amen-Renef** were/are represented. They were called the **neteru** (pronounced *net-er-oo*, singular: **neter** in the masculine form and **netert** in the feminine form).

The **neteru** (gods and goddesses) of ancient Egypt are personifications of function in action. Once a reference was made to the functions/attributes, each became a distinguishable agent; reflecting this particular function/attribute, and its influence on the world, such as God the Creator, God the First, God the Healer, ...etc.

Knot 2

Maat
The Queen of Harmony

In the Beginning - Chaos

Every Egyptian creation text starts with the same basic belief that before the beginning of things, there was a primeval endless abyss, without boundaries or directions, which they called **Nu/Ny/Nun**. This chaos possessed characteristics that were identified with four pairs of primordial powers/ forces. Each pair represents the masculine/feminine aspect that precedes creation.

Scientists agree with the ancient Egyptian description of the origin of the universe as being an abyss. Scientists refer to this abyss as *neutron soup* — the origin of all matter and energy in the universe. Such *chaos*, in the pre-creation state, was caused by the compression of matter, i.e. atoms did not exist in their normal states, but were squeezed so closely together, that many atomic nuclei were crowded into a space previously occupied by a single *normal* atom. Under such conditions, the electrons of these atoms were squeezed out of their orbits and move about freely (a degenerate state).

Nu/Ny/Nun is the "Subjective Being", the symbol of the *unformed, undefined, undifferentiated* energy/matter, inert or inactive, the uncreated state before the creation; it cannot be the cause of its transformation.

Law and Order

For the deeply religious people of Egypt, the creation of the universe was not a physical event (Big Bang) that just happened. The explosion (Big Bang) that led to the creation of the universe was an orderly event, unlike all other explosions that exhibit a random and disordered form.

The ancient Egyptian texts explain that all things that are to be created will be made by the will of **Amen-Renef** according to an orderly Divine Law that will govern the physical and metaphysical worlds. Setting the Law is referred to in the **Book of Knowing the Creations of Ra and Overcoming Apep** (Apophis).

> *"I had not yet found a place upon which I could stand. I conceived the Divine Plan of Law or Order (Maa) to make all forms. I was alone, I had not yet emitted Shu, nor had I yet emitted Tefnut, nor existed any other who could act together with me."*

Ma-at is the **netert** (goddess) that personifies the principle of cosmic order. The concept by which not only men, but also the **neteru** (gods) themselves were governed and without which the **neteru** (gods) are functionless. She signifies harmony, balance and equilibrium between all the different cosmic forces (**neteru**).

The Egyptians perceived the universe in terms of a dualism between **Ma-at** — Truth and Order — and disorder. **Amen-Renef** summoned the cosmos out of undifferentiated chaos, by distinguishing the two, by giving voice to the ultimate ideal of Truth. The forces of chaos were multitudiness and disorder, while the ideal Truth was a single harmonious entity, which is **Ma-at**, The Queen of Harmony.

Stay Tuned (Hear & Learn)

Egyptian creation texts repeatedly stress the belief of creation by the Word, i.e. that the world was manifested as a result of sound waves that were uttered by **Tehuti** (equivalent to *Hermes* or *Mercury*).

The harmony inherent in the geometry of forms was recognized early as the most cogent expression of a divine plan that underlies the world, a metaphysical pattern that determines the physical.

Ma-at, who is identified with the principle of order, equilibrium and cosmic harmony, is found not only in the innermost sanctuary of the temple but also as the decoration on the harp. The ancient Egyptian temple musicians had titles such as, **The Harpist of Maat, Mistress of the Neteru**, emphasizing the importance of **Ma-at** as the Queen of Harmony.

The Egyptians utilized the harmonic scale as the perfect instrument for teaching and demonstrating the workings of the cosmos. According to Plato, musical "theory" did exist in ancient Egypt, and was detailed by appropriate rules and laws. Plato [Laws, 656-7] states:

It appears that long ago [the Egyptians] determined on the rule ... that the youth of a State should practice in their rehearsals postures and tunes that are harmonically pleasing. These they prescribed in detail and posted up in the temples ... As regards music, it has proved possible for the tunes which possess a natural correctness to be enacted by law and permanently consecrated.

Plato admits clearly to the following points about ancient Egypt:
- learning music is important.
- harmonious (consonance vs. dissonance) notes are defined.
- detailed musical theory was prescribed.

Plato's *Collected Dialogues* also ascribed the knowledge of sound to the ancient Egyptians, in *Philebus [18-b,c,d]*:

SOCRATES: The unlimited variety of sound was once discerned by some god, or perhaps some godlike man; you know the story that there was some <u>such person in Egypt called Theuth</u>. He it was who originally discerned the existence, in that unlimited variety, of the vowels— not 'vowel' in the singular but 'vowels' in the plural—and then of other things which, though they could not be called articulate sounds, yet were noises of a kind. There were a number of them too, not just one, and as a third class he discriminated what we now call the mutes. Having done that, he divided up the noiseless ones or mutes until he got each one by itself, and did the same thing with the vowels and the intermediate sounds; in the end he found a number of the things, and affixed to the whole collection, as to each single member of it, the name 'letter.' It was because he realized that none of us could ever get to know one of the collection all by itself, in isolation from all the rest, that he conceived of 'letter' as a kind of bond of unity, uniting as it were all these sounds into one, and so he gave utterance to the expression 'art of letters,' implying that there was one art that dealt with the sounds.

The reference to *Theuth* above is the same *Theuth* mentioned in the *Phaedrus*, where we are explicitly told that he was an ancient Egyptian **neter** (god), *'the one whose sacred bird is called the Ibis'*, so as to exclude all doubt about his identity. It is obvious that his account is based on a genuine Egyptian tradition, because the ibis-headed **Tehuti** (Thoth) is an Egyptian **neter** (god).

Plato, in the *Philebus* [18-b,c,d], tells us (in his obscure way) that:

1.   The Egyptian **Tehuti** (Theuth/Thoth) was the first to

observe the *'infinity of sound'*.

2. **Tehuti** (equivalent to *Hermes* and *Mercury*) divided up the infinity of sound into three distinct categories. While all musical books talk about two forms of sound: *regular vibrations (pitch)* and *random vibrations (noise)*, **Tehuti** recognized *muting*, being the absence of sound, as a third element. Muting is a common skill employed by professional musicians so that notes and sound are contained in perfection.

3. **Tehuti** isolated the individual elements of sound in each of these categories *'until he knew the number of them'*.

4. **Tehuti** is the discoverer of the concept of letters, not necessarily as graphic, but as phonetic elements, i.e. each individual letter is a picture of its own sound (visual music).

5. Each "letter" is a unique unity that consists of its unique vibrational patterns.

Some examples of the waveform for different sounds are shown below.

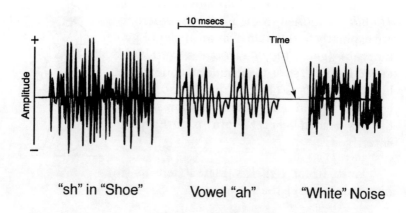

"sh" in "Shoe"   Vowel "ah"   "White" Noise

The presence of hieroglyphs in the shape of musical instruments (much older than 5,000 years) attest to their Egyptian origin.

By means of hundreds of various instruments that have been recovered, and by the many representations of musical scenes pictured in the tombs of noblemen from all periods, we know that from the Old Kingdom (4500 years ago) onwards, the Egyptians utilized musical scales, some of which are analogous to "Western" music. The positions of the harpists' hands on the strings clearly indicate ratios such as the fourth, the fifth, and the octave, revealing an unquestionable knowledge of the laws governing musical harmony.

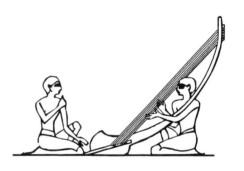

The oldest harps found in the sculptures are in a tomb, near the pyramids of Giza, about 4500 years old. The ratio between the longest and shortest string on these very old harps is around 1:3 to 1:4 (i.e., 1 to 2 octaves). Curt Sachs in his *Zweiklänge im Altertum,* 1929 [pgs. 168-70] concluded after his study of these old harps, that the ancient Egyp tians were capable of producing fifths, fourths, octaves, and unisons on these very early harps.

•   •   •

Flavious Josephus stated, in the 1ˢᵗ century of this era, in his volumes *The Jewish Antiquities,* that the ancient Egyptian temple priests used an enharmonic harp, meaning it was capable of producing a musical scale with ¼ tone.

In addition to the variation in the string lengths of the Egyptian harp, which produced ¼ tones, we find other ancient Egyptian musical instruments with such capability. The precise placement of frets (lateral ridges fixed across the fingerboard of a guitar, ...etc. to regulate the fingering) found in ancient Egyptian instruments are indicative of:

1. The geometric proportion of the musical chords and the knowledge of mathematical/geometrical ratios in music.

2. The smallness of the musical interval, as evident in the spacing between any two subsequent frets.

The found instruments corroborated previous evidence:

•   M. Villoteau, the French musician who accompanied Napoleon Bonaparte to Egypt over 200 years ago, described ancient Egyptian instruments (tambouras) with 25 frets, which are capable of producing ¼ tones.

•   Some Egyptian instruments in Turkish possession have up to 44 frets, which can produce even less than ¼ of a tone.

Musical instruments, with such close intervals as $1/3$, ¼, and even lesser, would require a high level of skill and intelligence to master. A $1/3$ tone or ¼ tone system provides more variation of harmony. Most people in the West have difficulty perfecting an instrument with the semitone system.

While we have to just take Western academia's word (i.e. no physical evidence) that the Greeks developed musical theory, the actual physical evidence is overwhelming that the ancient Egyptians knew musical theory that surpasses any others, past or present, thousands of years prior to the Greeks.

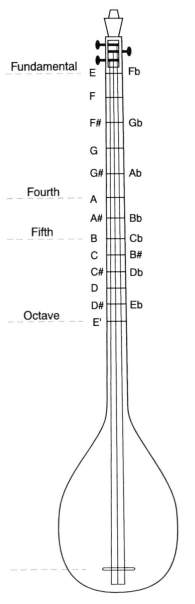

Fundamental   E   Fb
F
F#   Gb
G
G#   Ab
Fourth   A
A#   Bb
Fifth   B   Cb
C   B#
C#   Db
D
D#   Eb
Octave   E'

Ancient Egyptian instrument
showing some frets and their
correspondence to modern
musical notations.

The Principle Harmonic Law

As stated earlier, the ancient Egyptians believed that understanding music was the key to understanding the cosmos. The essential spirit of the perception of harmony is a tangible experience of the simultaneity of opposites (double inversion), which pervaded all aspects of Egyptian knowledge. Manifestation of these principles in different aspects of the ancient Egyptian civilization will be covered throughout this book. However, this principle law is best recognized in musical terms.

Music is pervaded by the fundamental law of reciprocity; changes in frequency and wavelength are reciprocal. Rising or falling tones, as reciprocal arithmetic ratios, are applied to string lengths. 'Major' and 'minor' are reciprocal tonal patterns.

Consider a string of a given length as unity. Set it vibrating; it produces a sound. Stop the string at its midpoint and set it vibrating. The frequency of vibrations produced is double that given by the whole string, and the tone is raised by one octave. The string length has been divided by two; and the number of vibrations per second has been multiplied by two: ½ has created its mirror opposite, $^2/_1$.

The relationship between the string-lengths for any two notes is the inverse of the relationship between their rates of vibration. For example, for the fifth, such as C to G (on the keyboard): the ratio between the two rates of vibration is 2:3 (260:390 Hertz), and that between the two string lengths required on any given instrument is 3:2. In other words, the harmonic proportion is the inverse (reciprocal) of every harmonic progression. The illustration above shows the musical root harmonies in vibrating strings and on the keyboard.

The arithmetic and harmonic proportions between the string lengths 1 and ½, representing the division of the vibrating string in half, produces the octave increase of fre-

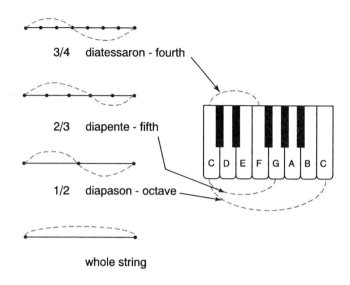

Musical root harmonies in vibrating strings and on the keyboard.

quency. This gives the progression 1 (fundamental), ¾ (fourth), $^2/_3$ (fifth), ½ (octave), because the harmonic mean between 1 and ½ = $^2/_3$, the musical fifth, and the arithmetic mean between 1 and ½ = ¾, the musical fourth. In comparing these two progressions, we see an inversion of ratios and a crossing of functional positions between the arithmetic and harmonic mean.

The presence of frets on the ancient Egyptian string instruments is sufficient evidence that the ancient Egyptians knew and implemented the geometric/arithmetic/harmonic relationship.

Play It By Heart

Beating time in music is quite important, because if a musician (not percussionist) falls out of time, the music sounds off and the ear tends to not listen and to drift. Rhythm has an effect on the heart and is measured against it as well.

Time beating could either be:

1 - Audible. In many musical representations in the ancient Egyptian monuments, musicians are accompanied by a person clapping to keep the musicians in time. How they would clap might depend on the time structure involved. In a simple 4 beat bar of music, the strongest beat will occur on the 1st and 3rd respectively, but the 2nd and 4th beats would be a snare (a clap almost) and these are almost like a release.

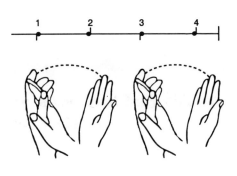

This resembles the beat of the heart — the pulse, and the relax.

2 - Silent. Time-beating with silent gestures was also used in ancient Egypt, in various ways. Ancient Egyptian time-beaters are shown giving signals, such as lifting the forearm, turning the palm either up or down, and stretching or doubling up the fingers.

Time-beaters are sometimes shown with one hand held partly out with thumb and forefinger forming a circle and other fingers held stiffly, while the other hand is placed on the ear or on the knee in a relaxed position, with the palm upward or downward. The thumb may be up, or bent against the forefinger.

Below are a few examples of silent time-beating as shown in tombs in Ta-Apet (Thebes).

•   •   •

As stated above, rhythm has an effect on the heart and is measured against it. In the epithets of a hymn to **Het-Heru** (who is identified with **Ma-at**), she is described as the **Lady of Intoxication, Lady of Music**. The ancient Egyptian word for *intoxication* is **tkh**. This same word also designates the *plumb bob*, shown below in the hand of **Heru** (Horus). The plumb bob determines the vertical and governs the equilibrium of

the scales. Scenes of weighing show that it is necessary to still the plumb line, because otherwise it would continue to oscillate.

Harmony is characterized by an unmistakable sense of 'equilibrium'. Equilibrium is a state in which positive and negative forces are balanced.

Tkh is also used to express everything that oscillates, titubates, or, by extension, wobbles — as in intoxication.

The plumb bob, tkh, is very often modeled in the form of the heart, ib, *The Dancer*. The heartbeat provides us with a convenient measure of time.

Knot 3

Ra, The One Joined Together

The One and All

In ancient Egyptian traditions, **Ra** personifies the primeval, cosmic, creative force. **The Litany** describes **Ra** as **The One Joined Together**, i.e., the One who is the All. The ancient Egyptian definition of **Ra** is the perfect representation of the Unity that comprises the putting together of the many diverse entities.

The Litany of Ra describes the aspects of the creative principle, being recognized as the **neteru** (gods) whose actions and interactions in turn created the universe. All the Egyptian **neteru** (gods) who took part in the creation process are aspects of **Ra**. There are 75 forms or aspects of **Ra**. As such, **Ra** is often incorporated into the names of other **neteru** (gods), such as in **Amen-Ra** of **Ta-Apet** (Thebes), **Ra-Atum** of **Onnu/Annu** (Heliopolis), **Ra-Harakhte** (shown herein), ...etc.

Ra-Harakhte

Creation is the sorting out (giving definition to / bringing order to) all the chaos (the undifferentiated energy/matter and consciousness) of the primeval state. All of the ancient Egyptian accounts of creation exhibit well-defined, clearly demarcated stages.

The Becoming One

The first stage was the self-creation of the Supreme Being as creator and Being. I.E., the passage from Subjective Being (**Nu/Ny/Nun**) to Objective Being (Atum). In simple human terms, this is equivalent to the moment that one passes from sleeping (unconscious state, subjective being) to being aware of oneself (gaining consciousness, objective being). It is like standing on solid ground.

Ra-Atum

This stage of creation was represented by the Egyptian sages as Atum rising out of **Nu/Ny/Nun**. In the *Pyramid Texts* there is the following invocation:

Salutation to thee, Atum,
Salutation to thee, he who comes into being by himself!
Thou art high in this thy name High Mound,
Thou comest into being in this thy name Khepri (Becoming One). [§1587]

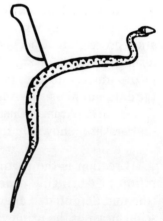

Next, the space/volume wherein the universe will be manifested must be established. The ancient Egyptian sages chose the twin serpents as the most flexible of all creatures, as the symbol for delineation of the universe. Yet, since the underlying law of creation is **Ma-at**, the ancient Egyptians added the feather of **Ma-at** to emphasize that the delineation of space and creation process will follow the **Ma-at** Law of harmony, balance, and equillibrium.

From Tomb of
Tut-Ankh-Amen

The Expanding Sacred Circle

The cosmic creative force, Ra, is written as a circle with a dot or point in the center. It is a circle moving in a circle, one and solitary. The circle symbolically represents the Absolute, or undifferentiated Unity.

The sacred circle of Ra must expand from the center outwards, in order to create the space that results from the Big Bang. The expansion (and later on contraction) of the universe is regulated by the Circle Index, i.e. the relationship between the diameter and the circumference of the circle.

The Circle Index is the functional representation of the circle. It is the ratio between the circumference of the circle to its diameter. It is popularized by Western academia by the Greek letter *pi* and given a value of 3.1415927.

The Circle Index and the Neb (Golden) Proportion were seen by the ancient Egyptians not in numerical terms but as emblematic of the creative or generative function. One cannot just reduce a process/function to a meaningless, unmeasurable "value", and then call it an "irrational number". The ancient Egyptians were not interested in abstract "number gymnastics".

The ancient Egyptians rarely used the sacred circle in Egyptian architecture. The circle bounds creation but is not the manifested creation. The inscribed polygonal shapes within the circle are the manifested creation. That the ancient Egyptians knew how to inscribe a polygon within a circle is proven beyond doubt by their invention of capitals and column shafts that are polygonal in cross section.

Like the ancient Egyptians, Kepler considered the circle's relationship to figures derived from it and relationships among these figures themselves by constructing the polygon in a circle. Kepler regarded the property of being knowable as a criterion of nobility, indicating the closeness of a figure's relation to the circle, and thus its fitness to contribute to the archetype.

The Egyptians built their capitals with nine elements and occasionally with seven, in addition to 6, 8, 11, and 13-sided polygons, because they knew the properties of the circle and its relationship to perpendicular coordinates and other geometric figures. Their executed work is sufficient evidence of such knowledge.

The Egyptians manifested their knowledge of the circle properties and other curves, as early as their surviving records. A 3rd Dynasty (~ 2630 BCE) record shows the definition of the curve of a roof, in Saqqara, by a system of coordinates. This shows that their knowledge of the circle en-

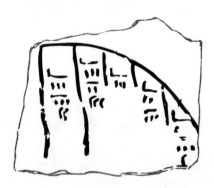

abled them to calculate the coordinates along this vertical curve. Accordingly, the construction workers followed precise dimensions in their executed circular curves.

Such application was evident in Egypt at least 2,000 years before Archimedes walked this earth.

The Ennead, The Nine Circles

In the ancient Egyptian texts, Atum came into being out of **Nun**, the primeval waters (unpolarized groundstate of matter). This initial act of self-creation then produced the **Annu/Onnu** (Heliopolitan) Ennead (group of nine). Atum spat out the twins Shu and Tefnut, who in turn gave birth to Nut and Geb, whose union produced **Ausar** (Osiris), **Auset** (Isis), **Set** (Seth) and **Nebt-Het**(Nephthys).

The nine aspects of the Grand Ennead emanate from,

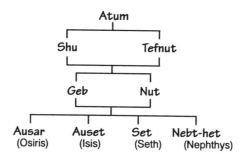

and are circumscribed about, The Absolute. They are not a sequence, but a unity — interpenetrating, interacting, interlocked. They are the generator of all creation, as symbolized in **Heru** (Horus), who according to the **Leiden Papyrus**, Stanza No. 50, is:

> "**the offspring of the nine-times-unity of neteru**".

Heru (Horus) is also associated with the number five (as will be explained later). Five is the number of the cosmic solids (polyhedrons): tetrahedron, cube, octahedron, dodecahedron, and icosahedron. These five solids are formed from within nine concentric circles, with each solid touching the sphere which circumscribes the next solid within it. These nine circles represent the nine — unity of the Ennead, the generator of all creation that is represented by these cosmic solids.

The Musical Proportions in the Circle

Kepler, who clearly stated that his works were the resurrection of ancient Egyptian knowledge [see pg. 17], sought
the origins of musical harmonies in the archetypal forms of
geometry; in fact, in the division of the circle by the vertices
of regular polygons (dividing the circle into different numbers of equal arcs, which is equivalent to constructing the
sides of regular polygons inscribed in it).

The circle is imagined to be opened out into a string. A
string stretched out straight can be divided in the same way
as when it is curved around into a circle — it is divided by
the side of the inscribed figure, i.e. the generation of musical
ratios among the arcs of a circle.

Kepler only accepted polygons that could be constructed
with a straight line and compass. A harmonic proportion
could be produced by a division of the circle only if the parts
formed ratios with the whole and with each other that be-
longed to a constructible polygon.

A straight line can be divided into any given rational
ratio, i.e. in any ratio that can be expressed in the form $a{:}b$
where both a and b are integers. If the whole string is divided into parts such that they are individually in consonance
both with each other and with the whole, the division is called
harmonic.

• • •

The eight notes that form the function of nearly all
chords, i.e. unison (1:1), octave (1:2), fifth (2:3), fourth (3:4),
major third (4:5), minor third (5:6), major sixth (3:5), and
minor sixth (5:8), were explained as divisions of a circle as
follows:

- The 1:1 proportion, which is identity, is called unison.

- The diameter divides the circumference into the ratio 1:2, the octave.

- The equilateral triangle divides the circumference into the ratio 2:3, the musical fifth.

- The square divides the circumference into the ratio for 3:4, the musical fourth.

- The pentagon divides the circumference into the ratios 4:5 and 3:5.

- The hexagon divides the circumference into the ratio 5:6.

- The octagon divides the circumference into the ratio 5:8, the minor sixth.

Neb: The Golden Segment

Neb is an ancient Egyptian term meaning *gold* (traditionally, the finished perfected end product, the goal of the alchemist), *Lord, master*.

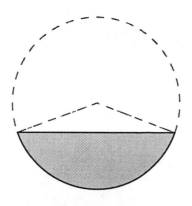

The hieroglyph denoting Neb is a segment of a circle, whose central angle is 140°. The ratio of this angle to the whole circle (length of arc to whole circumference) = 0.3889, which constitutes the second power of 0.625. The second power spiritually constitutes reaching to a higher level. Neb means exactly that.

Later, we will find how 0.625 is used in ancient Egyptian design as the ratio of 5:8, and that 5 and 8 are important numbers in the Summation (so-called *Fibonacci*) Series as well as in the Neb (Golden) Proportion (so-called ϕ).

Knot 4

Tehuti,

The Divine Deliverance

Let Creation Begin

Creation is the act of the transformation of **Nun** from its undifferentiated state to differentiated energy/matter (things, objects, thoughts, forces, physical phenomena). Transformation (differentiation) is achieved through sound (the Word) as the prime mover (creative agency) of the inert energy/matter. The agent of this action is **Tehuti**, The Divine Tongue, whose creative words generated the related spiral patterns of nature.

Tehuti

Egyptian creation texts repeatedly stress the belief of creation by the Word. The Egyptian **Book of the Coming Forth by Day** (wrongly and commonly translated as the *Book of the Dead*), the oldest written text in the world, states:

> *I am the Eternal ... I am that which created the Word ... I am the Word ...*

In ancient Egypt, the *words* of **Ra**, revealed through **Tehuti** (equivalent to *Hermes* or *Mercury*), became the things and creatures of this world, i.e. the words (meaning soundwaves) of the Creator that created the elements of the universe.

The *word* (any word) is scientifically a vibrational complex element, which is a wave phenomenon, characterized by movement of variable frequency and intensity, between oppositely charged poles.

Sound is caused by compressing air particles, by rearranging the spacing and movement of air particles, i.e. creating forms. There is a direct relationship between wave frequency and form. As a result, sound waves have different geometrical forms, such as the waveforms shown here.

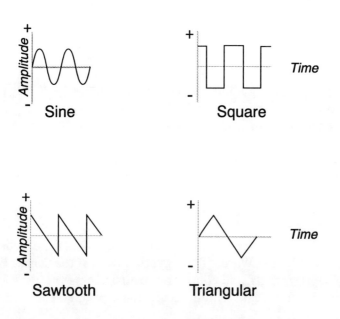

Each waveform is the result of its particular sound. Likewise, the ideal form of writing and speaking should be a form mirroring its sound.

Metu Neter

The ancient Egyptians called their language **Metu Neter**, meaning *word of **neter** (god)/good*. The Egyptian term is indicative of the unity of speech and script, i.e. sound and form.

Plato's *Collected Dialogues* also affirms the ancient Egyptian intent of their language, in *Philebus* [18-b,c,d]:

...he [Tehuti] conceived of 'letter' as a kind of bond of unity, uniting as it were all these sounds into one, and so he gave utterance to the expression 'art of letters,' implying that there was one art that dealt with the sounds.

The ancient Egyptians did not use words as we do, that is, as symbols or sounds linked together, which have fixed, memorized associations and which we compose in sequential patterns within the mind.

Given the importance of chants, spells, and a person's name in ancient Egypt, it is clear that the sound of the words must have had a functional connection with their meanings. For them, words were of a musical nature; or, more precisely, speaking was a process of generating sonar fields establishing an immediate vibratory identity with the essential principle that underlies any object or form.

The image of each Egyptian symbol contained its specific vibrational pattern. Words were constructed of these symbols in a manner incorporating and amplifying the meaning of the individual symbols, so that the meaning of a word emerged from the interplay of symbols, as the meaning of a chord or a musical phrase results from the combination of notes.

The Egyptian names of things often contained keys to their interrelatedness. The structure of the words followed the principles of connection, distinction and inversion that lie at the root of creation. The fundamental law of reciprocity/inversion applies also to word structure. Here are a few examples:

A. Neb means *gold* (traditionally the finished perfected end product, the goal of the alchemist), Lord, master.

Ben (neb spelled backwards), means *opposition, it is not* and *there is not*. It also means the *primordial stone*, (the first state of matter), i.e. the opposite of the perfected *(gold)*.

B. Akh: spirit, spirit-state, be, become a spirit, glorious splendid, etc.
Kha: (Akh spelled backwards) corpse.

C. Rkh: know, aware of, knowledge.
Khr: (Rkh spelled backwards) fall.

D. Sia: knowledge, intelligence.
Ais: (Sia spelled backwards) viscera.

E. Hetep: stillness, peace.
Ptah: (Hetep spelled backwards) rearranging, forming (active).

Please note that the vowels shown in the middle of a word are only approximations of sounds. One should follow the arrangement of the "consonants".

[More about hieroglyphs in Knot 9, *The Hieroglyphic Mysticism*.]

Squaring the Circle: The Perfect Tone

The word (sound) energies of **Tehuti** transformed the creation concept (symbolized in a circle) into a physical and metaphysical reality. Such transformation is reflected in the ancient Egyptian process of "squaring the circle", as evident in all their "mathematical" papyri. In all these papyri, the area of a circle was obtained by squaring the circle. The diameter was always represented as 9 cubits. The ancient Egyptian papyri equate the 9 cubit diameter circle to a square with the sides of 8 cubits.

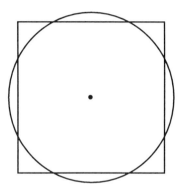

The number 9, as the diameter, represents the Ennead, the group of 9 **neteru** (gods) who produced the ingredients of creation. The 9 are all aspects of **Ra**, the primeval cosmic creative force, whose symbol is/was the circle.

8 corresponds to the physical world as we experience it. 8 is the number of **Tehuti,** and at **Khmunu** (Hermopolis), **Tehuti** is known as the **Master of the City of Eight**.

Musically, the ratio 8:9 is the Perfect Tone. The 8:9 ratio is present in ancient Egyptian works, such as the proportion of the inner chamber of the top sanctuary at Luxor Temple.

The Octave Sets the Tone

In Egypt, the well-known text, *Coffin of Petamon* [Cairo Museum item no. 1160], states:

I am One who becomes Two,
who becomes Four,
who becomes Eight,
and then I am One again.

This new unity (One again) is not identical, but analogous, to the first unity (I am One). The old unity is no longer, a new unity has taken its place: *The King is Dead, Long Live the King*. It is a renewal or self-replication. And to account for the principle of self-replication, 8 terms are necessary.

Musically, the renewal theme of 8 terms corresponds to the *octave* because it reaches through all eight intervals of the scale (the eight white keys of the keyboard).

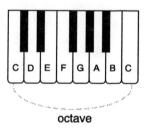

octave

For example, an octave is 2 successive Cs (*Do's*) on a musical scale, as illustrated herein on the keyboard.

The experience of hearing the octave contains the mystery of a simultaneous sameness and difference.

As stated earlier, **Tehuti** (Hermes to the Greeks, Mercury to the Romans) was/is called *Master of the City of Eight*. **Tehuti** gives man access to the mysteries of the manifested world, which is symbolized by Eight.

Knot 5

Seshat, The Enumerator

Number Mysticism

The **netert** (goddess) Seshat is well described in numerous titles which ascribe two main types of activities to her. She is **The Enumerator, Lady of Writing(s), Scribe, Head of the House of the Divine Books** (Archives).

The Enumerator

The other aspect of Seshat and obviously closely related to it is one where she is described as the **Lady of Builders**. [More about this aspect of Seshat in Knot 11.]

The divine significance of numbers is personified in ancient Egyptian traditions by Seshat, The Enumerator.

The ancient Egyptians had a "scientific and organic system" of observing reality. Modern-day science is based on observing everything as dead (inanimate). Modern physical formulas in our science studies almost always exclude the vital phenomena throughout statistical analyses. For the ancient Egyptians, the whole universe is animated.

Animism is the concept that all things in the universe are animated (energized) by life forces. This concurs, scientifically, with the kinetic theory, where each minute particle of any matter is in constant motion, i.e., energized with life forces.

In the animated world of ancient Egypt, numbers did not simply designate quantities but instead were considered to be concrete definitions of energetic formative principles of nature. The Egyptians called these energetic principles *neteru* (gods).

For Egyptians, numbers were not just odd and even — they were male and female. Every part of the universe was/ is a male or a female. There is no neutral (a thing). Unlike in English, where something is he, she, or it, in Egypt there was only he or she.

These animated numbers in ancient Egypt were referred to by Plutarch, in *Moralia Vol V*, when he described the Egyptian 3-4-5 triangle:

The upright, therefore, may be likened to the male, the base to the female, and the hypotenuse to the child of both, and so Ausar [Osiris] may be regarded as the origin, Auset [Isis] as the recipient, and Heru [Horus] as perfected result. Three is the first perfect odd number: four is a square whose side is the even number two; but five is in some ways like to its father, and in some ways like to its mother, being made up of three and two. And panta *[all] is a derivative of* pente *[five], and they speak of counting as "numbering by fives". Five makes a square of itself.*

The vitality and the interactions between these numbers shows how they are male and female, positive and negative, vertical and horizontal, ...etc.

The ancient Egyptian mode of calculation had a direct relationship with natural processes, as well as metaphysical ones. Even the language employed in the Egyptian papyri serves to promote this sense of vitality, of living interaction. We see this understanding as an example in Item no. 38 of the papyrus known as the **Rhind Papyrus**, which reads,

"I go three times into the hekat (a bushel, unit of volume), a

seventh of me is added to me and I return fully satisfied."

Numbers were animated and personified. Likewise, calculations were personal in ancient Egypt. We are part of this natural process called the universe. Even in our present-day, we hear the genius among us describe how they *feel* the subject of their excellence. They live their work in order to excel and exhilarate.

Egyptians manifested their knowledge of number mysticism and harmonical proportions in all aspects of their lives, such as art and architecture, as will be explained throughout this book. The evidence that Egypt possessed this knowledge is commanding. As examples:

1. The heading of the ancient Egyptian papyrus known as the **Rhind** (so-called "Mathematical") **Papyrus** (1848-1801 BCE) reads,

   "Rules for enquiring into nature and for knowing all that exists, every mystery, every secret".

   The intent is very clear that ancient Egyptians believed and set the rules for numbers and their interactions (so-called mathematics) as the basis for "all **that exists**". Egyptological academia misses the forest AND the trees — splitting hair over what they perceive as merely mathematical exercises. What is even worse, is that these academicians have no knowledge of the practical application of "mathematics" in real life.

   Squaring the Circle, as detailed in the previous chapter, is a prime example of the Egyptian number mysticism in the Egyptian papyri.

2. The famous ancient Egyptian hymn of **Leiden Papyrus J**

350 confirms that number symbolism had been practiced in Egypt, at least since the Old Kingdom (2575-2150 BCE). It is a rare direct piece of evidence of the Egyptian knowledge of the subject. The Leiden Papyrus consists of an extended composition, describing the principle aspects of the ancient creation narratives. The system of numeration, in the Papyrus, identifies the principle/aspect of creation and matches each one with its symbolic number.

This Egyptian Papyrus consists of 27 stanzas, numbered from 1 to 9, then from 10 to 90 in tens, then from 100 to 900 in hundreds. Only 21 have been preserved. The first word of each is a sort of pun on the number concerned.

The numbering system of this Egyptian Papyrus by itself is significant. The numbers 1 to 9, and then the powers 10, 20, 30, etc., now come to constitute the energetic foundations of physical forms.

3. All the design elements in Egyptian buildings (dimensions, proportions, numbers, ...etc.) were based on the Egyptian number symbolism, as will be shown throughout this book.

4. The ancient Egyptian name for the largest temple in Egypt, namely the Karnak Temple Complex, is **Apet-sut**, which means **Enumerator of the Places**. The temple's name speaks for itself. This temple started in the Middle Kingdom in ca. 1971 BCE, and was added to continuously for the next 1,500 years. The design and enumeration in this temple are consistent with the number symbolism of the physical creation of the universe.

5. The **netert** (goddess) Seshat is described as the **Enumerator**, as early as the known dynastic history of Egypt, i.e. at least 5,000 years ago.

The Egyptian concept of number symbolism was subsequently popularized in the West by and through the Greek Pythagoras (ca. 580-500 BCE). It is a known fact that Pythagoras studied for about 20 years in Egypt, soon after Egypt was open to Greek *exploration* and *immigration* (in the 7th century BCE).

Pythagoras and his immediate followers left nothing of their own writing. Yet, Western Academia attributed to him and the so-called *Pythagoreans*, an open-ended list of major achievements. They were issued a blank check by Western academia.

Pythagoras and his followers are said to see numbers as divine concepts, ideas of the God who created a universe of infinite variety, and satisfying order, to a numerical pattern.

The same principles were stated more than 13 centuries before Pythagorus' birth, in the heading of the Egyptian's Rhind Papyrus, which promises,

"Rules for enquiring into nature and for knowing all that exists, every mystery, every secret".

Fraction Mysticism

All Egyptian thought, science, and other disciplines devolve from the concept of the mystical Primordial Scission. This starting point of creation is mentioned in every subject and practically in every document. It is not idle talk, they were always focused on the beginning point, for one does not know where one is going to, if one does not know where one comes from.

The natural consequence of the division of unity into multiplicity was the principle of double inversion. The ancient Egyptian mathematical method itself is a practical application of such a principle.

To Egypt, a fraction — any fraction — could only be a fraction of *unity*. Esoterically, because all numbers are to be regarded as divisions of unity, the mathematical relationship a number bears to unity is a key to its nature.

Ancient Egypt would state, **"one seventh and a seventh and a seventh"**, but our familiar idea of $^3/_7$ did not exist in the mind of the Egyptian.

The ancient Egyptians represented fractions, i.e. having a numerator of 1, by drawing the mouth of **Ra** as the numerator and unit marks underneath for the denominator.

To write $^1/_7{}^{\text{th}}$, the Egyptian simply wrote the numeral 7, in an upside-down form, underneath the **mouth of Ra's** symbol. A seventh is called **Ra-Sefhet** = mouth of seven. The glyph might be translated as 'One emits seven'.

Heading each ancient Egyptian numerological (so-called *mathematical*) papyrus that has been found, there is a table of the division of 2 by odd numbers from 3 to 101, similar to our tables of logarithms and square roots, in which all fractions with a numerator of 2 are broken down into constituent fractions with a numerator of 1, which reduces the time spent for calculation. So, in practice, the Egyptian system was no more laborious than ours, and may have been less so.

With the sole exception of $^2/_3$, no fraction was ever written which had a numerator greater than unity. This exception has an exceptional esoteric reason, since $^2/_3$ is not a fraction but a bond [see Knot 6].

The Generation Law (Proportioned Progression)

In order to create the dynamics necessary for progression and extension from the Unity, an assymmetrical division is needed. The ancient Egyptian representation of $^1/_2$ clearly shows sides of unequal length, indicative of asymmetrical division. The obvious, rational method of illustrating one-half, for symmetrical divisions, would be to make the sides equal.

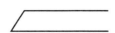

Glyph for 1/2.
Glyph for Ma-at.

The glyph for Ma-at is the same as the glyph for $^1/_2$, indicative of the Ma-at Law of assymetric division.

The natural law of generation is achieved through harmonically proportioned progression. This natural progression follows a series that is popularized in the West as the "Fibonacci Series", which is a summation series. Since it was in existence before Fibonacci (born in 1179 CE), it should not bear his name. Fibonacci himself and his Western commentators, did not even claim that it was his "creation". Let us call it as it is — a Summation Series.

The Summation Series is a progressive series, where you start with a number, say 1, then you add this number to its preceding number. From any two successive terms, all others may be constructed by simple moves of the compass, i.e., 1, 1, 2, 3, 5, 8, 13, 21, 34, 55, 89, 144, and so on.

The Summation Series was known to the ancient Egyptians, and it was the origin of ancient Egyptian harmonic design.

- Many ancient Egyptian plans of temples and tombs, throughout the dynastic history of ancient Egypt (as will

be shown throughout this book), show along their longitudinal axis and transversely, dimensions [in the Egyptian cubits of 1.72' (0.523 m)] that follow consecutive
terms of the Summation Series 3, 5, 8, 13, 21, 34, 55, 89,
144, . . .

This practice went as far back (at least) as the Pyramid
(erroneously known as *mortuary*) Temple of **Khafra**
(Chephren) at Giza, built in 2500 BCE (about 3,700 years
before Fibonacci) shows that the essential points of the
temple comply with the Summation Series. [See analysis of
this temple on page 140-41.]

• The Summation Series conforms perfectly with, and can
  be regarded as an expression of, Egyptian mathematics,
  which has been defined by everyone as an essentially additive procedure.

  This additivity is obvious in their reduction of multiplication and division to the same process by breaking up
  higher multiples into a sum of consecutive duplications.
  It involves a process of doubling and adding. This progressive doubling lends itself to speedy calculation. It is
  significant that the methods used in modern calculators
  and computers are closer to the Egyptian method.

• Egyptian folk songs show rhythms that are considered to
  be musically additive. Their customary clapping of hands
  and/or wooden and ivory clappers (hundreds of them
  were found in the ancient tombs), as well as their beating
  of drums, gave to the Egyptian melody the intricate pattern of additive rhythm in asymmetrical groups of small
  units. In such patterns, the Egyptians followed breath-
  ing rhythms that were uneven and additive.

  The Egyptian melody progresses from a note x time units
  long, to another note y time units long. The sum of x and

Clapping by Clapper and Hand

y forms the metrical pattern to be repeated again and again like the in-and-out of respiration. There might be three or four such notes in a pattern; but they can easily be reduced to two members, representing one, tension, and one, relaxation.

•   •   •

The Summation Series in musical terms can be easily observed by looking at the pattern of the keyboard. There are 8 white keys and 5 black keys. These black keys are in groups of 2's and 3's.

The series 2:3:5:8 is the beginning of the Summation Series.

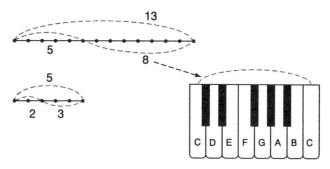

Summation Series on the Keyboard

As the Summation Series progresses, the ratio between successive numbers tends towards the **Neb** (Golden) Proportion. This proportion has recently been assigned an arbitrary name by Western academia — the Greek alphabet letter φ (phi), even though it was known and used long before the Greeks. And what is worse is that there is not even factual evidence that the Greeks knew it at all!

Integrity and honesty demand that an ancient Egyptian term be used for this proportion, i.e. **Neb** (Golden) Proportion. **Neb** has the most appropriate meaning, in function, since it means *gold, divine*. This proportion is also known in Western texts as *Golden* and *Divine*.

Western academia has even misrepresented the **Neb** (Golden) Proportion by calling it the *Golden Number*. A proportion is not a number, it is a relationship. Number implies the capacity to enumerate.

The term *golden section* did not come into use in Western texts until the 19th century. In most Western mathematical books and journals, the common symbol for the **Neb** (Golden) Proportion is *tau* (τ) instead of *phi* (presumably because *tau* is the initial letter of the Greek word for *section*).

•   •   •

The Egyptians knew and used the Summation Series at least 4,500 years ago — as well as its derivative, the **Neb** (Golden) Proportion. This knowledge was also reflected in the proportion of human figuration, as incorporated into their artwork. Ancient Egyptians followed a precise canon of proportion, which Plato attested to its remoteness of age:

"That the pictures and statues made ten thousand years ago, are in no one particular better or worse than what they now make."

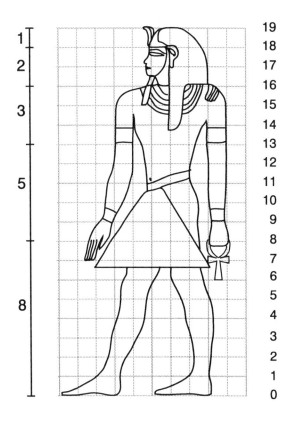

Human Figuration On an Original Ancient Egyptian Grid

Practical Mathematics in Ancient Egypt

The numerous monuments of ancient Egypt, with their perfect construction, attest to their superior knowledge, among other things, of mathematics and geometry.

The ancient Egyptians never formulated or worked out problems for their own sake (so-called *Greek mathematics*). To do so would be an exercise in vanity and useless number gymnastics.

•   •   •

The Egyptians had a system of decimal numbering, with a sign for 1, another for 10, 100, 1000 and so on. The evidence at the beginning of the 1st Dynasty (2575 BCE) shows that the system of notation was known up to the sign for 1,000,000.

All that is known of Egyptian "mathematics" comes from a Middle Kingdom papyrus and a few fragments of other texts of a similar nature. The study of mathematics began long before the found "mathematical" papyri were written. These found papyri are not a mathematical treatise in the modern sense, that is to say they do not contain a series of rules for dealing with problems of different kinds, but merely a series of tables and examples worked out with the aid of the tables. The four most referred to papyri are:

1. The Rhind "Mathematical" Papyrus (now in the British Museum) is a copy of an older document during King Nemara (1849-1801 BCE), 12th Dynasty. It contains a number of examples to which academic Egyptologists have given the serial numbers 1-84.

2. The Moscow "Mathematical" Papyrus (in the Museum

of Fine Arts of Moscow) also dates from the 12th Dynasty. It contains a number of examples to which academic Egyptologists have given the serial numbers 1-19. Four examples are geometrical ones.

3. The Kahun fragments.

4. The Berlin Papyrus 6619, which consists of four fragments reproduced under the numbers 1-4.

•   •   •

Below, is a synopsis of the contents of the Rhind "Mathematical" Papyrus:

- Arithmetic
  - Division of various numbers.
  - Multiplication of fractions.
  - Solutions of equations of the first degree.
  - Division of items in unequal proportions.

- Measurement
  - Volumes and cubic content of:
      cylindrical containers
      rectangular parallelopi pectal

- Areas of:
      squaring the circle
      rectangle
      circle
      triangle
      truncated triangle
      trapezoid

- Batter or angle of a slope of a pyramid and of a cone.

- Miscellaneous problems:
  - Divisions into shares in arithmetical progression.
  - Geometrical progression.

Other Mathematical Processes known from other Papyri include:

- Square and square root of quantities involving simple fractions [Berlin 6619].

- Solution of equations of the second degree [Berlin Papyrus 6619].

● ● ●

It must be noted that the Rhind Papyrus shows that the calculation of the slope of the pyramid [Rhind Nos. 56-60] employs the principles of a quadrangle triangle, which is called the *Pythagoras Theorem*. This Egyptian Papyrus is dated thousands of years before Pythagoras walked this earth.

The so-called *Pythagorean Theorem* should be called the Heru (Horus) "Theorem", because Heru symbolizes the hypotenuse in the ancient Egyptian traditions of the 3:4:5 triangle. [See Knot 8 for additional information].

The theorem states that the square of the hypotenuse of a right triangle is equal to the sum of the squares of the other two sides. The 3:4:5 triangle represents this rule by using integer numbers for all three sides.

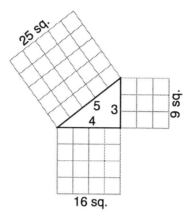

The square of side 3 = 9 squares.

The square of side 4 = 16 squares.

The square of side 5 = 25 squares.

The total of both squares (3 and 4) = 9 + 16 = 25 squares, which is the square for the hypotenuse side.

The 3:4:5 triangle is as ancient as Egypt is.

•   •   •

We should not judge the level reached by the Egyptians in mathematics, because our only knowledge in this field is based on two incomplete papyri and a few fragments, almost all of which date from the Middle Kingdom. Moreover, we should not cavalierly ignore the objective of the papyri as stated at its beginning, which is the mystical aspects of numbers, fractions, and calculations.

Knot 6

The Two Parts, Setting the Tone

The Pair of Ra's Lips

The hieroglyphic sign known as the "mouth of Ra" denotes unity. It is derived geometrically from two intersecting circles. As such, it symbolizes a balancing consciousness between two complementary pairs of opposites that are needed to cause creation and its continuance.

When analyzing the geometry of this Egyptian hieroglyph, we find that the centers of the two circular curves form equilateral triangles.

The equilateral triangle is related to **Tehuti** [see Knot 8].

In ancient Egypt, the *words* of **Ra**, revealed through **Tehuti** (equivalent to *Hermes* or *Mercury*), became the things and creatures of this world.

The geometry of the Egyptian hieroglyphs reflected this relationship between **Ra** and **Tehuti**.

Neheb-Kau, The Provider of Forms

In the **Khmunu** (Hermopolis) traditions, the pre-creation subjective realm consists of 4 pairs (male and female) of attributes. The females of the pairs are represented as human-headed serpents with their legs tied, indicative of their essential nature as being *action*, but while in the subjective realm (before creation) they are *inert, not moving*.

The serpent represents the spiral movement induced by the creative word of **Tehuti** (Thoth). The serpent, as a metaphor for the spiral, is the hieroglyphic symbol used to represent the **netert** (goddesses). The female aspect, the **netert** (goddess), represents the active potent power in the universe.

One of the most used ancient Egyptian hieroglyphs is the spiral. Many of the key words dealing with some aspect of creativity are written with the spiral. We find it in:

A̲u̲sar's(Osiris) name;
Hekau̲, word of power;
Kheperu̲, creations;
Heru̲ (Horus), first power of creation [see pg 82]

The same symbol was used to denote the number 100 in ancient Egypt.

Neheb Kau — meaning *the provider of forms, qualities, attributes* — was the name given to the serpent representing the primordial spiral in ancient Egypt. **Neheb Kau** is depicted as  a two-headed serpent, emphasizing the dual spiral nature of the universe. **Neheb Kau** shows that the ancient Egyptians knew that there was a connection between spirals and the patterns underlying nature.

The Spitting Image: Shu & Tefnut

The world, as we know it, is held together by a law that is based on the balanced dual nature of all things (wholes, units). This principle was first expressed in the ideas of Shu and Tefnut — the representation of husband and wife — the characteristic Egyptian way of expressing duality and polarity. This dual nature was manifested in ancient Egyptian texts and traditions, for the Self-Created Atum:

...didst spit out as Shu, and didst spit out as Tefnut. [Pyramid Texts §1652].

This is a very powerful analogy because we use the term "spitting image" to mean exactly like the origin. Shu and Tefnut represent the sameness, since they are both the spitting images of the Self Creator. At the same time, Shu and Tefnut, as a male and a female, signify polarity, i.e. the otherness.

Tefnut   Shu

In an ancient Egyptian text (Bremner-Rhind Papyrus), the Master of the Universe declared the concept of duality:

I was anterior to the Two Anteriors that I made, for I had priority over the Two Anteriors that I made, for my name was anterior to theirs, for I made them anterior to the Two Anteriors ...

This declaration is symbolized in the Egyptian hieroglyph of the twin spiral, as shown here.
Patterns generated by spirals moving in opposite directions (one clockwise, the other counterclockwise) are frequent in nature, like the pattern of the florets of a daisy.

The Two Parts of Trinity

According to ancient Egyptian texts and traditions, the Self-Created **neter** (god), Atum, spat out Shu and Tefnut then placed his arms round them, and his **Ka**, entered into them. As a result, an intimate relationship/bond was established between the Self Creator (Atum) and the Two-Parts (Shu and Tefnut). It is the Three that are Two that are One. This action generated the First Trinity.

In the ancient Egyptian texts, Shu and Tefnut are described as the ancestors of all the **neteru** (gods/goddesses) who begat all beings in the universe. This triangulation of Atum-Shu-Tefnut ensured a continuous relationship between the Creator and all subsequent created. It also served as the model of subsequent regeneration — the typical combination of building blocks of the universe. It allowed a continuous chain of triangulation of all subsequent generation and regeneration.

The bond of the Two Parts to their Origin is reflected in the ancient Egyptian symbol for $^2/_3$. The ancient Egyptians called $^2/_3$ **The Two Parts**, and it was never considered to be a fraction. The Two Parts are shown unequal in length, and are attached to the symbol of Unity.

The sign for $^2/_3$ indicates an aspect of unity itself, one of the direct simultaneous consequences of the Primordial Scission. Unity is proportioned as 2 is to 3.

In the Summation Series (1, 2, 3, 5, 8, 13, ...), the ratio between the two subsequent numbers of 2 and 3 provides the highest reciprocal pulsation in the Series at 0.667. This powerful relationship of 2:3 is the primary basis for all creation in the universe, as will be shown in the following pages.

The Musical Fifth (Heavenly Marriage)

Two symbolizes the power of multiplicity, the female, mutable receptacle, while Three symbolizes the male. This was the 'music of the spheres', the universal harmonies played out between these two primal male and female universal symbols of **Ausar** (Osiris) and **Auset** (Isis), whose heavenly marriage produced the child, **Heru** (Horus). Plutarch confirmed this Egyptian wisdom in *Moralia Vol V*:

Three (Osiris) is the first perfect odd number: four is a square whose side is the even number two (Isis); but five (Horus) is in some ways like to its father, and in some ways like to its mother, being made up of three and two. And panta *(all) is a derivative of* pente *(five), and they speak of counting as "numbering by fives".*

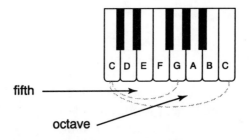

Musically, the ²/₃ interval on the vibrating string and on the keyboard determines the vibration of the perfect fifth, reaching through five intervals (as shown above). It is the first harmonic interval, to which all other harmonic intervals relate.

The multiplication of 2 (**Auset**) and of 3 (**Ausar**) gives us all the numbers for the tuning system by successive multiplication by fifths (2:3), **Heru**.

The Heru Golden Star (The Pentagon)

Since the relationship between 2 and 3 is the building block of Five, the number five in ancient Egypt was written as two (II) above three (III), or as a five-pointed star (shown below).

The Egyptian five-pointed star forms the corners of the pentagon, which is harmoniously inscribed in the Sacred Circle of Ra. The Star was the Egyptian symbol for both destiny and the number five. The five-pointed stars were the homes of departed souls, as stated in the Unas (wrongly known as *Pyramid*) Texts, Line 904,

be a soul as a living star.

The Egyptian 5-pointed stars are found all over ancient Egyptian tombs and temples, throughout its history.

• • •

All phenomena without exception are polar in nature, treble in principle. Therefore, five is the key to the understanding of the manifested universe, which Plutarch explained in the Egyptian context,

...And panta *(all) is a derivative of* pente *(five)...*

The above statement is also descriptive of the five cosmic solids (tetrahedron, cube, octahedron, dodecahedron, and icosahedron). These five polyhedrons are drawn within nine concentric circles, with each solid touching the sphere which circumscribes the next solid within it. These are the nine — Unity of the Ennead, the generator of all creation.

Knot 7

The Generative Square Roots

The Root Rectangles

The role of a root in a plant is the same exact role/function as that of the root in geometry. The root of a plant assimilates, generates, and transforms energies to the rest of the plant. The roots symbolize the constant, creative process of acting and reacting energy.

Likewise, the geometric root is an archetypal expression of the assimilative, generating, transformative function and process, whereas fixed whole numbers are the structures that emerge to build upon these principles of process.

As stated earlier, the concept of creation was manifested in the act of squaring the sacred circle of Ra.

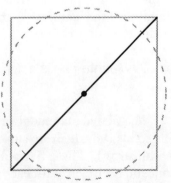

The square is the basic geometric shape from which all root rectangles can be generated.

The diagonals serve as the generators of root rectangles.

When we start with a square whose side is one, the diagonal is $\sqrt{2}$. From the square root of two, other root rectangles are produced directly by simply drawing with compasses, i.e. applying sacred geometry, producing without measurement — by using squares and rectangles and their diagonals.

The ancient Egyptians were able to obtain root rectangles without measurements through various ways such as:

•   Start with a square that is a 'root 1' rectangle. The next, the $\sqrt{2}$ rectangle, is produced from the square by setting the compass at the length of the diagonal and producing the base line to meet it. This makes the length of the long side equal to the square root of 2, taking the short

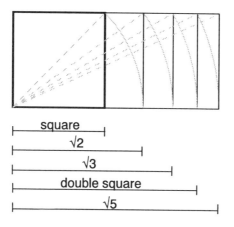

side as unity. The $\sqrt{3}$ rectangle is produced from the diagonal of this rectangle, and so on.

- Within a square on the wall or on the ground, the ancient Egyptians were able to easily generate dynamic design by obtaining the root rectangles. [See some applications on pages 123-7.]

In the square shown below, a diagonal is drawn from 0 to C. From corner 0, an arc is drawn between A and B.

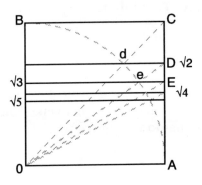

Arc AB and diagonal 0C intersect at point d. The horizontal line dD determines the $\sqrt{2}$ line.

A line from 0 is extended to D. The intersection (e) of this new diagonal 0D and the AB arc determines the location for $\sqrt{3}$, by the horizontal line eE.

From the intersection of 0E and the arc AB at point e, we can determine the $\sqrt{4}$ line, i.e. the double-square.

By following the same procedures, we can obtain $\sqrt{5}$, ...etc.

•   •   •

Design that is based on root rectangles is called *generative dynamic design*, which only the Egyptians practiced. Egyptian sacred objects and buildings have geometries based upon the division of space attained by the root rectangles and their derivatives, such as the **Neb** (Golden) Proportion, as will be shown throughout this book.

• • •

From the roots of Two, Three, and Five, all harmonic proportions and relationships can be derived. The interplay of these proportions and relations commands the forms of all matter, organic and inorganic, and all processes and sequences of growth.

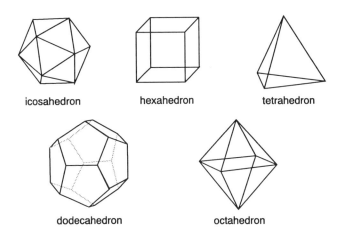

icosahedron   hexahedron   tetrahedron

dodecahedron   octahedron

The three sacred roots are all that are necessary for the formation of the five cosmic solids (shown above), which are the basis for all volumetric forms, where all edges and all interior angles are equal. The manifestation of these five volumes are generated from the Egyptian Ennead [see page 41].

The Double Square (The Musical Octave)

As stated earlier, the circle is the archetype of creation in ancient Egypt. Dividing the circle by its diameter produces the 1:2 ratio, which is the musical octave. The manifested world through this division is symbolized by the inscribed two equal squares, representing the balance between our physical and metaphysical worlds. [see diagram below]

The 1:2 geometric outline of the twin-squares represents the diapason, the octave. As stated on page 50, the octave represents renewal or self-replication.

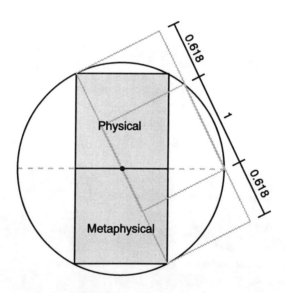

In Egyptian architectural design, the 1:2 double square rectangle assumed great importance in the elements or the general outline of the plan. Such outlines represented the octave and served as the renewal place for the physical and metaphysical well-being of the King.

- The earliest surviving of such 1:2 rectangular complexes is the Zoser Complex (2630-2611 BCE) at Saqqara. This vast sanctuary is in the form of a double square (1,000 x 500 cubits), whose walls are oriented exactly along the cardinal directions. It contains the Step Pyramid, several buildings, colonnades, and temples.

  It was a very active site for all successive Pharaohs. The main function of the Zoser sanctuary was to serve as the **Heb-Sed** site.

  Heb-Sed was the most important festival from the point of view of the Kingship. Being a divine medium, the Egyptian King was not supposed (or even able) to reign unless he was in good health. The **Heb-sed** festival was a rejuvenation of the King's vital force.

  The **Heb-Sed** Festival took place at regular intervals during the King's life.

  This vast sanctuary set the pattern for later holy places, in Egypt and elsewhere.

- The Festival Hall (**Akh-Menu**) of Tuthomosis III at the Karnak Temple was used for his **Heb-Sed** Festival. It also consists of double-square outlines. It is interesting to note that it is shaped like a tabernacle. [See illustration of its column capitals on pages 158-9.]

- On the vertical plane, the doorways of the ancient Egyptian temples were also proportioned 1:2 [see pgs 164-5].

The **Neb** (Golden) Proportion is obtained by using a rectangle with sides of 1:2. This comes from the diagonal that transverses the two worlds, indicated by the upper and lower squares: the world of spirit and the world of body — the root-five diagonal.

The Root Five Rectangle

The root-five diagonal of the 1:2 rectangle is also the diagonal that divides the archetypal creation circle into two halves. The top half of the circle contains the manifested physical creation, as represented by the inscribed square (*BCFG* below).

The manifested square divides the root-five diagonal into **Neb** (Golden) proportioned parts (*X* and *Y* below). As a result, the root-five diagonal provides two reciprocal **Neb** (Golden) rectangles: *ACFH* (1 x 1.618) and *CDEF* (1 x 0.618), or a square plus two lateral **Neb** (Golden) rectangles. The root 5 rectangle is *ADEH*, containing the two above-mentioned combinations.

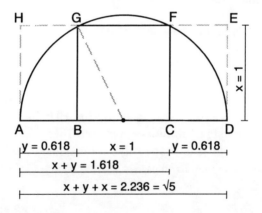

The inscribed square in the upper half of the circle represents the physical manifestation of the world. The resultant proportions were essential parts of the ancient Egyptian design, as will be shown throughout this book.

Such symbols (the square and half circle) are two of the hieroglyphic symbols in Ptah's name.

The three symbols of Ptah's name in hieroglyphs consists of: the square *P*, the half circle *T*, and a three-looped/knotted/united rope *H*. The symbols are shown below, separately and together (superimposed) as one unit.

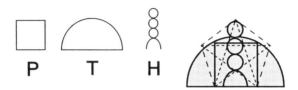

The superimposition of all three symbols shows the outline of the 5-pointed Egyptian star, and henceforth the pentagon, which brings to mind Plutarch's explanation of the Egyptian context:

...And panta *(all) is a derivative of* pente *(five)...*

In ancient Egypt, Ptah is/was the Cosmic Architect, the cosmic shaping force, the giver of form (smith). He is/was the patron of crafts, trades, and the arts. He is/was the co-agulating, creative fire. His job is to give form to the words of **Ra** as spoken by **Tehuti** (Thoth), according to the Laws of balance and equilibrium (**Ma-at**). Therefore, Ptah sits enthroned or stands upon a pedestal in the form of the glyph for **Ma-at** (cosmic law, harmony, equilibrium).

Ptah

The Greeks identified Ptah with Hephaestus, the divine smith. Their names may be linked etymologically. He is also identified with the Romans' *Vulcan.*

The Neb (Golden) Rectangle

The two rectangles *ACFH* and *BDEG* [page 78] produce the perfect ratio of the **Neb** (Golden) Proportion and its reciprocal 0.618. These rectangles are proportioned very closely to the 5:8 rectangle. 5 and 8 are the first two numbers in the Summation Series (1,1,2,3,5,8,13,21,...), whose ratio ($^5/_8$ = 0.625) comes closest to 0.618. The difference between 0.618 and 0.625 is 0.007 — a negligible difference for its use in harmonic design. The 5:8 is therefore called the **Neb** (Golden) rectangle.

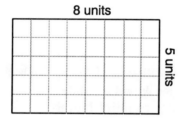

8 units

5 units

A 5:8 rectangle shown on the typical
ancient Egyptian grid system

5 is the number of **Heru** (Horus) in the divine triangle 3:4:5, and 8 is the number of **Tehuti** (Thoth), known in **Khmunu** (Hermopolis) as the *Master of Eight*. The 5:8 represents the relationship between **Heru** and **Tehuti**.

In ancient Egypt, *intelligence* was identified with the heart and personified as **Heru** (Horus) — the seat of the conceiving mind, the conscience. *Will* was identified with the tongue and personified as **Tehuti** (Thoth) — the seat of creative intellectual utterance.

As per the Shabaka Stele (8th century BCE), all **neteru** (gods), and each part/organism in the universe, are given a heart and a tongue with hidden powers, in order to remember the primeval creation and to visualize the persistence of the Creator's work.

The heart and tongue are personified by **Heru** and **Tehuti**, who operate as a duo in many situations in ancient Egyptian representations. As an example, they are shown in the symbolic Tying of the Two Lands. [Another representation is shown on page 127.]

Tehuti   Heru

The Whirling Squares Spirals

We do not hear simple quantitative differences in soundwave frequencies, but rather the logarithmic, proportional differences between such frequencies. The inner ear is shaped like a logarithmic spiral, to correspond to the way we hear. That spiral shape was noted in Egyptian medicine and jewelry.

Logarithmic expansion is the basis of the geometry of spirals. The fetus of man and animals, which are the manifestation of the generation laws, are shaped like the logarithmic spiral. Manifestations of spirals are evident in vegetable and shell growth, spider webs, the horn of the dall sheep, the trajectory of many subatomic particles, the nuclear force of atoms, the double helix of DNA, and most of all, in many of the galaxies. Patterns in the mental realm, as well, are also generated in spiraling motions.

The Leiden Papyrus, Stanza No. 50, describes **Heru** as

"the offspring of the nine-times-unity of neteru".

Heru (Horus), the New One, at number 10 is therefore the first power of 1. This is the law of nature, since the logarithm of 10 = 1.

•   •   •

The logarithmic spiral is the product of the combined effect of addition and multiplication, which is a progressive addition, just like the Summation (Fibonacci) series (1,1, 2, 3, 5, 8, 13, 21, 34...).

As stated earlier, Egyptian mathematics is essentially additive procedures, where multiplication was converted into a process of doubling and adding.

A logarithmic spiral is formed by progressive addition, by means of "whirling squares", consisting of squares and **Neb** (golden) rectangles growing in harmonic progression from center *0* outward. Each consecutive stage of growth is encompassed by a **Neb** (golden) rectangle that is by a square larger than the previous one.

You start with a square *0 1 2 3*. Then you add the **Neb** (Golden) rectangle *4 5 1 0*, whose sides are at a 5:8 ratio. Continue the same process, as indicated below.

squares	+ **Neb** (Golden) rectangles	= **Neb** (Golden) rectangles
0 1 2 3	+ 4 5 1 0	= 4 5 2 3
7 4 3 6	+ 4 5 2 3	= 7 5 2 6
8 9 5 7	+ 7 5 2 6	= 8 9 2 6
9 10 11 2	+ 8 9 2 6	= 8 10 11 6 etc.

Since logarithmic spirals follow the same process as the Summation Series, they are subsequently characterized by the **Neb** (Golden) Proportion. The two dashed diagonals (like all diagonals of the compounded **Neb** rectangle) are in **Neb** (Golden) ratio to each other (1.618).

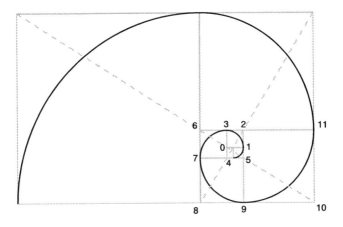

A logarithmic spiral indicated by "whirling squares".

Logarithmic spirals can also be built by whirling triangles that make use of an isosceles triangle that has a top angle of 36°, i.e. by dividing the circle into 10 divisions.

•   •   •

Analysis of the Egyptian bas-relief composition shows that its designer not only proportioned the picture but also the groups of hieroglyphs by the application of whirling square rectangles to a square, i.e. spiral. [See example on pages 126-7.]

The mystery of musical harmony that develops out of a simultaneous inversion also contains a simultaneity of addition and multiplication (which produces the logarithmic function). The octave of a musical fundamental is achieved by the addition of the intervals: in string lengths the fifth plus the fourth equals the octave, and also the multiplication of the vibrational frequencies of the fourth and the fifth equals the octave ($^4/_3$ x $^3/_2$ = 2).

● ● ●

The use of logarithmic spirals were abundant in ancient Egypt, indicative of their representations of all growth patterns in the universe. In addition to the examples discussed on page 67, we find the logarithmic spiral shown on the red crown of ancient Egypt. This crown represents the solar (in broader terms than just the sun) principle that is the generative matrix that is called Ra.

Knot 8

Triangles, The Building Blocks

Sound/Forms of Triangles

The physical and metaphysical role of Three is recognized in the many trinities of ancient Egypt. These trinities are/were the building blocks that began with the triad, Atum-Shu-Tefnut, which set the tone as the typical universal building block. It was the beginning of the universal triangulation — the continuous chain that maintained a connecting relationship between the Creator and the created. Each unity has a *triple power* and a *double nature* — active and passive.

For the ancient Egyptians, Three/Triads/Trinities/Triangles are one and the same. There was no difference between geometric triangles, musical triads, or any of the numerous trinities of ancient Egypt. The clearest example was explained by Plutarch regarding the 3:4:5 triangle, as will be shown on pages 88-89. For now, let us check Plutarch's statement in *Moralia Vol V*:

> *The Egyptians hold in high honor the most beautiful of the triangles, since they liken the nature of the Universe most closely to it...*

In other words, triangles in their different forms represent different natures in the universe. The same principle applies to sound/music. As stated earlier, **Tehuti** (Thoth) recognized for the ancient Egyptians the unlimited variety of sound into three categories: consonances, dissonances, and mutes.

Students of modern music are often taught that intervals and triads (major, minor, augmented, and diminished) are the building blocks for composing music.

As stated earlier, forms are the manifestation of sound variations, and triangles are its basic, simplest form.

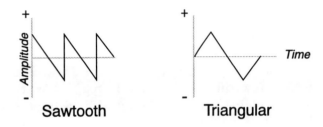

Sawtooth   Triangular

Triads were an essential part of the ancient Egyptian civilization. Each small locality had its own triad. These local triads were not in conflict with each other — they were the building block of each locality.

On a larger scale, we are familiar with numerous ancient Egyptian triads, such as:

> Amen - Mut - Khonsu
> Ausar(Osiris) - Auset(Isis) - Heru(Horus)
> Ptah - Sekhmet - Nefertum
> Ptah - Sokar - Ausar (Osiris)

The following is an overview of the geometric configuration of three Egyptian triangles.

The Tehuti (Ibis) Triangle

Plutarch, in his *Moralia Vol V* about ancient Egypt, wrote:

By the spreading of Ibis' feet, in their relation to each other and to her bill, she makes an equilateral triangle.

Ibis is the sacred bird of Tehuti (Thoth), whose words created the world. The symbol denoting the mouth of Ra is geometrically constructed from equilateral triangles. [See Knot 6.]

An equilateral triangle could be set out with the Egyptian rope knotted at twelve equal intervals and wound about four pegs, so that it formed three sides, each measuring four units.

The line joining from any corner to the middle of the opposite side is its perpendicular. With the Egyptian cord, all perpendiculars can be established without any measurements whatsoever.

Musically, the Ibis (equilateral) Triangle, in relation to its circumscribed circle, provides the ratio 2:3, the musical fifth. Therefore, both the shape and sound of this triangle were/ are described as the most beautiful.

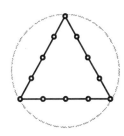

The Ausar (Union) Triangle

The 3:4:5 triangle, where the height is to the base as 3 is to 4, was called the "Osiris" Triangle by Plutarch. This triangle was set out with the Egyptian rope, wound about three pegs so that it formed three sides measuring three, four, and five units, which provides a 90° angle between its 3 and 4 sides.

It is a historical lie to call it the *Pythagorean Triangle*. It was used in ancient Egypt for thousands of years before Pythagoras walked this earth.

It is very clear from Plutarch's testimony below, that the ancient Egyptians knew that 3:4:5 is a right-angle triangle, since 3 is called **upright** and 4 is the **base**, forming a 90° angle.

Plutarch wrote about the 3:4:5 right-angle triangle of ancient Egypt in *Moralia, Vol V*:

The Egyptians hold in high honor the most beautiful of the triangles, since they liken the nature of the Universe most closely to it, as Plato in the Republic *seems to have made use of it in formulating his figure of marriage. This triangle has its upright of three units, its base of four, and its hypotenuse of five, whose power is equal to that of the other two sides. The upright, therefore, may be likened to the male, the base to the female, and the hypotenuse to the child of both, and so Osiris may be regarded as the origin, Isis as the recipient, and Horus as perfected result. Three is the first perfect odd number: four is a square whose side is the even number two; but five is in some ways like to its father, and in some ways like to its mother, being made up of three and two. And* panta *(all) is a derivative of* pente *(five), and they speak of counting as "numbering by fives". Five makes a square of itself.*

The 3-4-5 right-angle triangle has major significances, some of them being:

1 -   It represents the perfect union (matrimony) of male and

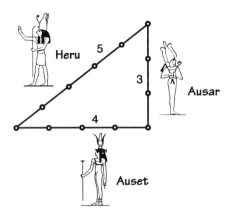

female principles.

2 - It represents the cyclical nature of the universe, of life/
death/resurrection/renewal. As Plutarch stated,

> *... since they [Egyptians] liken the nature of the Universe most closely to it.*

Ausar (Osiris) died and was resurrected, to become **Heru**
(Horus), The New One.

3 - It is a relatively simple task to lay out rectangles and
other more complex geometrical figures, after laying out
the 3:4:5 triangle. [See examples on pages 18-19.]

4 - Musically, the consonance of the 3:4 proportion, i.e.
Ausar:Auset, of the **Ausar** Triangle is called the *fourth*.
3:4 is the arithmetic musical mean between 1 and ½.

Musically, the ratio of 3:2 is the fifth, the number of
Heru. $^2/_3$ is the harmonic mean between 1 and ½.

[More information on this triangle is mentioned in Knots 5 and 6.]

The Neb (Golden) Triangle

The 5:8 isosceles triangle, where the height is to the base as 5 is to 8, is by far the most widely used in constructional and harmonic diagrams in Egyptian architecture and art, and it was no whim for Viollet-le-Duc to call it the **Egyptian Triangle**.

The dimensions of the 5:8 triangle are actually the first two consecutive terms of the Summation Series (3, 5, 8, 13, 21, 34, 55, 89, . . .) that approximate the **Neb** (Golden) to a theoretical "deviation" of 1%, which is inconsequential in building application.

Numerous Egyptian amulets, representing the mason's level, have been discovered and are now scattered through-

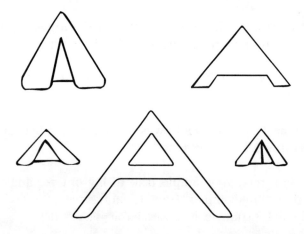

out the museums of the world (Turin, Louvre, ...etc.). The 5:8 triangle represents the greatest percentage of these shapes that included the 3:4:5 right-angle triangle and equilateral triangle.

Musically, the ratio 5:8 represents the minor sixth [see page 44].

Another less-known property of the 5:8 triangle is its very close approximation to the isosceles triangle, which may be inscribed within a heptagon, so that its vertex extends to $^3/_{14}$ of the circumscribing circle. The angle at the base of the 5:8 triangle is 51° 20' 25" and its vertex angle is 77° 19' 10", while those of the triangle inscribed within a heptagon are, respectively 51° 25' 43" and 77° 8' 34". The discrepancy is 10' 36", 360 = 0.00048. The triangle within the heptagon is practically the same as the 5:8 one.

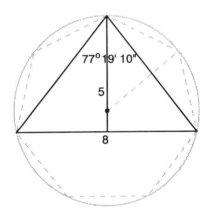

The 5:8 triangle can be established by the use of the Egyptian Sacred Cord. Firstly, the 3:4:5 triangle is established, then the upright is extended for two additional units, as shown herein.

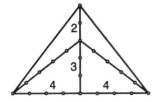

The Egyptians designed capitals of columns with seven elements. Their architects used the 5:8 triangle for such a purpose.

Knot 9

The Hieroglyphic Mysticism

The Corruption of Hieroglyphs

The ancient Egyptians' way of writing was in existence before Egypt's known dynastic history. Their mode of writing is commonly called *hieroglyphs*, which comprises a large number of pictorial symbols. The word *hieroglyph* has its origin in the Greek, and means *holy script* (*hieros* = holy, *glyphein* = impress).

The relationship between the sound and form of the ancient Egyptian symbols was discussed in Knot 4.

All the signs of hieroglyphs are images from the Egyptian natural world, and therefore it was of an Egyptian origin and not imported or influenced by other cultures.

In the 12th Dynasty (2000-1780 BCE), about 700 signs were in more or less constant use. There are practically unlimited numbers of these natural symbols.

Academic Egyptologists cavalierly chose 24 symbols out

of hundreds of hieroglyphs, and called them *alphabets*, then they gave various "functions" to the other hundreds of symbols such as "syllabic", "determinative", etc.

Deciphering the ancient Egyptian language began with Champollion (ca. 1822), but practically ended then. He made some assumptions to unlock the mysteries of the ancient Egyptian language. Later, Egyptologists carelessly made more and more assumptions. They kept piling assumptions on top of assumptions. They made up rules as they went along. The end result was chaos. One can easily see the struggle of academia to understand the ancient Egyptian language, which reached a dead end, as is reflected in an apparent "deciphering" of no more than 1500 words that have contradictory and confusing meanings.

Even if we accept that these 1500 words and terms are correctly deciphered, this number is less than 1% of the vocabulary listed in an average English language dictionary. With such a small fraction of a vocabulary, it is impossible to make any rational, coherent sense out of the Egyptian writings.

The Metaphysical Symbols

Academic Egyptologists go against all the historical evidence when it comes to their simplistic view of the ancient Egyptian hieroglyphs, such as:

• Besides hieroglyphs, the ancient Egyptians had two known non-pictorial forms of writing — so-called *hieratic* and *d emotic* scripts. Ancient Egyptians never abandoned hieroglyphs for the non-pictorial form of writing. So the pictorial form of writing was called Holy Script by the Greeks because it is/was a holy (metaphysical) script, and not a form of primitive alphabet, as portrayed by academic Egyptologists.

- The metaphorical and symbolic concept of the hieroglyphs was unanimously accepted by all early writers on the subject. Samples will be shown below.

- Plato's *Collected Dialogues* refers to the ancient Egyptian writing mode in *Philebus* [18-b,c,d]:

  > ...he [Tehuti] found a number of the things, and affixed to the whole collection, as to each single member of it, the name 'letter.' ... he [Tehuti] conceived of 'letter' as a kind of bond of unity, uniting as it were all these sounds into one, and so he gave utterance to the expression 'art of letters,' implying that there was one art that dealt with the sounds.

  It is obvious from the context above, that Plato/Socrates here speaks about letters as graphic elements, but his use of the word *'letters'* does not necessarily imply that he considered Tehuti (Thoth) the inventor of a proper alphabet in our sense of the word, but as the divine essence.

- In his treatise on Auset (Isis) and Ausar (Osiris), which is one of the most instructive sources for our understanding of the Greek conception of Egyptian religious ideas, Plutarch mentions the hieroglyphs and their metaphorical and mythological significance in several places. In his *Moralia Vol V*, Plutarch states,

  > The babe is the symbol of coming into the world and the aged man the symbol of departing from it, and by a hawk they indicate God, by the fish hatred, and by the hippopotamus shamelessness.

  In Plutarch's opinion, the allegorical method used here illustrated the basic principle of hieroglyphic writing, which is a pictorial expression of divine ideas and sacred knowledge.

- Plutarch listed an extensive number of distinguished Greeks who at different times visited Egypt. Among them is also mentioned Pythagoras, whose admiration and dependence on *the symbolic and occult teachings of the Egyptians'* is emphasized and illustrated by a comparison of the allegorical method used in the so-called Pythagorean precepts, and *'the writings that are called hieroglyphs'.*

- Chairemon lived in Alexandria before he went to Rome where he was the tutor of Nero from 49 CE onward. Chairemon described 19 hieroglyphs in his books, followed by an explanation of the allegorical significance of each.

- Diodorus of Sicily, in his *Book I*, stated:

  Their — the Egyptians' — writing does not express the intended concept by means of syllables joined one to another, but by means of the significance of the objects that have been copied, and by its figurative meaning that has been impressed upon the memory by practice. For instance they draw the picture of a hawk, a crocodile ... and the like. Now the hawk signifies to them everything which happens swiftly, since this animal is practically the swiftest of winged creatures. And the concept portrayed is then transferred, by the appropriate metaphorical transfer, to all swift things and to everything to which swiftness is appropriate, very much as if they had been named. And the crocodile is a symbol of all that is evil.

- Clement of Alexandria about 200 CE gave an account

of the hieroglyphs. The metaphorical and allegorical qualities of the hieroglyphs are at the same time explicitly mentioned, and his examples are expounded in the same symbolic way as those of earlier writers.

• Plotinus stated that:

The Egyptians, either by exact science or spontaneously, had arrived at a method by means of which they could write with distinct pictures of material objects, instead of ordinary letters expressing sounds and forming words and phrases. These pictures were not merely ordinary images of the things they represented, but were endowed with certain symbolic qualities (sophia), by means of which they revealed to the initiated contemplator a profound insight into the very essence and substance of things, and an intuitive understanding of their transcendental origin, an insight which was not the result of reasoning or mental reflection, but was acquired spontaneously by means of divine inspiration and illumination. As artistic representations of the phenomenal objects, they revealed, in fact, the ideal world of the soul.

Geometric Proportion of Hieroglyphic Symbols

As explained many times earlier, the ancient Egyptian language contains an intimate relationship between sound and form. The sound waveforms, as shown on page 46, illustrate regular geometric forms for different sounds.

The Egyptian hieroglyphs are perfect geometric shapes that were drawn with a prescribed proportion. Academic Egyptologists assigned silly names to these sacred scripts, such as a *loaf* when referring to a perfectly formed half circle.

The following are samples of obvious geometrically pro-portioned hieroglyphic symbols showing circles or parts thereof, squares, spirals, rectangles, and triangles, as well as intersecting and compounding of these shapes.

Each form has its meaning that is manifested in its pro-portioned geometry.

The proportionality of these symbols must be analyzed harmonically, as to the relationship between sound and physical form, and the metaphysical significance of each symbol.

An interesting observation regarding the significance of the differently proportioned rectangles is found on the pylon at the Temple of Khonsu, at Karnak. This pylon shows the falcon, vulture, and ibis, each on a differently proportioned rectangle.

- The falcon of **Heru** (Horus) stands on a 1:2 rectangle, which represents the octave — a self-replication.

- The vulture represents Mut, the assimilative power. Therefore, the ratio between the sides of the rectangle is the square root of the **Neb** (Golden) Proportion.

  The roots are symbols of pure archetypal, assimilative, generating, and transformative processes. [See Knot 7.]

- The ibis symbol of **Tehuti** (Thoth) is atop a **Neb** (Golden) rectangle 5:8.

Knot 10

Harmonic Proportion
of Human Figuration

Canon of Proportion

It is well known and accepted that all Egyptian art and architecture, including representations of the human figure, followed a precise canon of proportion. Plato attested to the remote age of the canon of properties:

"That the pictures and statues made ten thousand years ago, are in no one particular better or worse than what they now make."

The Egyptian artistic representation is essentially two-dimensional. When representing three-dimensional objects on a plane surface, the Egyptians avoided using perspectives, and maintained a two-dimensional profile, with the exception of a few parts of the body.

The early records from the 5th Dynasty (2465-2323 BCE) show a vertical line of reference for the human figure used as an axis, with significant points marked on the axis and symmetrically about it [see opposite page]. The highest defined point along the vertical axis is the hairline on the forehead.

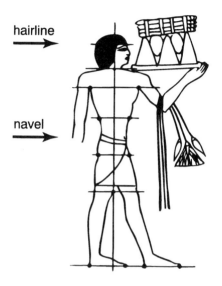

One of several offering-bearers with guidelines and dots.
Tomb Chapel of Manufer, Saqqara, 5ᵗʰ Dynasty.

This total height of the standing earthly human (excluding the crown of the head) is 6 times the width of the foot.

Records found from after the 5ᵗʰ Dynasty were set out upon a grid of squares (equivalent to our graph paper) that made it easier to determine the precise proportions. As such, the vertical (or horizontal) proportions can be read in terms of the number of squares (or fraction thereof) in the grid.

About 100 such grids are preserved, some dating from the Old Kingdom. Egypt through the Old, Middle, and New Kingdoms operated on a grid of 18 squares to the standing earthly man's forehead. The foot occupied 3 squares.

The Divine and Earthly Realms

As stated earlier, the oldest discovered records from the 5th Dynasty show that the highest defined point along the vertical axis is the hairline of the person's head, when presented in the earthly realm.

Egyptian figurations carefully mark — with a headband, crown, diadem, or joint — a dividing line for the top of the skull of the earthly man, thus separating the crown of the skull. [See man on right, opposite page.] The height of the body was measured exclusive of the crown. The illustrations show the earthly man as always higher than the divine aspects [such as Tehuti, in the illustration on the opposite page].

The representation of the neteru (gods/goddesses) and/ or human beings *in the afterlife* are shown on an 18-square grid, for the full height to the top of the head.

The choice of the number 18 is very significant and is consistent with all other ancient Egyptian aspects. In the Unas Funerary (so-called *Pyramid*) Texts, the Divine Man (King) is generated from 2 x 9, i.e. 18 divine units:

'The King [symbol of the Divine Man] **came forth from between the thighs of the two divine Nines'**

The difference in the height between the two realms reflects the ancient Egyptian deep understanding of the physiology and the role of humans on earth.

The removal of this part of the human brain leaves man alive, but without discernment, hence with no *personal* judgement. The person is in a vegetated state, i.e. living and acting only as the executant of an impulse that he receives, without actual choice. It is like a person in a coma.

The earthly being must use his cerebral instrument to choose his actions. These actions will be in agreement or at

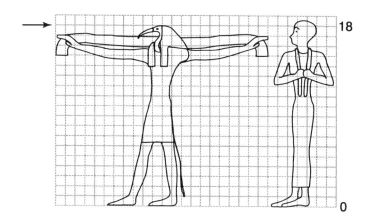

Tehuti (above) illustrates both the vertical (18-grid squares) and the horizontal stretched arm-span (fathom), measuring 22-square grid.

variance with natural harmony. If during his/her earthly life the actions are not harmonious with nature, s/he will reincarnate again to the earthly realm, to try another time.

When the earthly man has developed his consciousness to the utmost perfection, he will no longer need his cerebral instrument. The perfected soul will receive from **Ausar** (Osiris) a favorable judgement:

Let the deceased depart victorious.

The perfected soul will go through the process of trans-formation and the subsequent rebirth, and as the Egyptian writing describes it,

becomes a star of gold and joins the company of Ra, and sails with him across the sky in his boat of millions of years.

The Descriptive Proportion

The ancient Egyptian canon for the harmonic proportion of human figures differed only between children and
adults. The differences were reflective of the actual physical differences at these two stages.

At birth, it is the *navel* that divides the height of child
into two halves. Upon maturation (reaching puberty), the
junction of both legs (reproductive organs) is at mid-height
of the adult figure. The position of the navel now divides the
height into unequal parts that make the parts and the whole
in compliance with the **Neb** (Golden) Proportion.

The navel is located at about 11.1 grid squares, from the
bottom of the heel on the 18-square grid system (or the same
equivalent ratio 0.618 for grid or non-grid systems). Such
division follows the laws of harmony between the two parts
themselves, and the parts to the whole, as per the following
two relationships:

1 - The ratio between the Two (top and lower) Parts of the
divine height are harmonic.

Top	:	Lower	is	0.618
Lower	:	Top	is	1.618

2 - Between the Two Parts to the whole Unity (divine
height) — taking the full height (to the hairline of the
earthly man's head) as 1, the body from the feet to the
navel, in the Egyptian canon, is equal to the reciprocal
of the **Neb** (Golden) Proportion, i.e. 0.618. The portion
from the navel to the hairline of the head equals the
power 2 of the reciprocal of the **Neb** (Golden) Proportion, i.e. 0.382.

$$^1/_N + {^1/_{N^2}} = 1$$
$$0.618 + 0.382 = 1$$

Because of the intimate relationship between the Summation Series and the **Neb** (Golden) proportion, we find that
the different parts of the figure also follows the Summation
Series [See Knot 5].

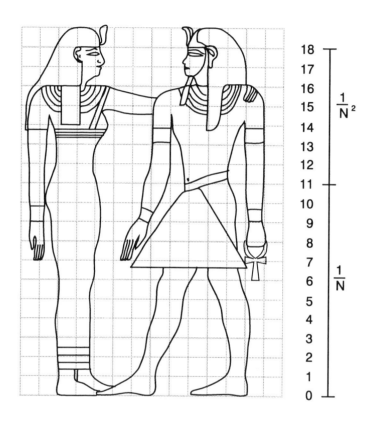

Original Grid in KV22 of Amen-hotep III

Not all essential points that determine the harmonic proportion of the figure were integer numbers, many such points (such as the navel) were located at fractions of a grid square. Another example is the precise location of the armpit at the 14 $^2/_5$ line on the typical 18-square grid. Such a line is even shown on the 5th Dynasty record as a significant point, on and about the vertical axis [see illustration on page 101]. Records of smaller subdivisions of grid squares have been found. [See illustration on page 121.]

•   •   •

The canon of proportion also applied to other positions, such as sitting, as shown on this found ancient Egyptian papyrus. In such a case, the total height of the sitting figure was always 14 grid-squares, to the hairline on the forehead.

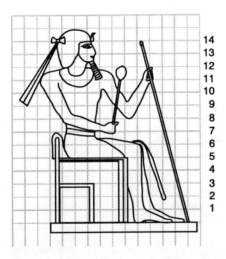

14
13
12
11
10
9
8
7
6
5
4
3
2
1

All other items on the ancient Egyptian walls of temples and tombs followed precise rules of proportion, as well.

•   •   •

There is a very scant and questionable record that has been assigned to the end of the Late Kingdom, of using a grid of 22 squares. Notwithstanding the weakness of such a claim, all agree that there is no evidence that the ancient Egyptians stopped using the 18-square grid at any time. But more importantly is the fact that when using a vertical axis and significant points (5th Dynasty), grids of 18 squares, or even the questionable few grids of 22 squares, the human representation followed the same proportion between the different parts of the human figuration.

In harmonic proportion, measurements are not an issue. Harmonic proportion is the relationship/ratio between the parts to the whole.

Knot 11

Seshat, The Builder

The Knowledge Manifestation

As stated earlier, the **netert** (goddess) Seshat is well-described by numerous titles that ascribe two types of activities to her. She is the **Enumerator: Lady of Writing**(s), **Head of the House of the Divine Books**, **Head of the House of Books** (Archives).

The other aspect of Seshat and closely related to it is the one where she is described as the **Lady of Builders**.

Builders, artisans, sculptors, and painters were part of a team that adhered rigidly to the pre-ordained canons of proportion. Their positions can be compared with that of modern designers of printed circuitry or microprocessors, who are constrained within a technological framework of function that depends absolutely upon the laws of electronics.

The ancient Egyptian knowledge that manifested itself in their monuments was prescribed into technical specifications that were kept in archives throughout the country. Many of these documents made their way to the Library of Alexandria; some survived and many more were destroyed as heretic writing, by self-righteous religious zealots.

The Written Building Specifications

Ancient Egyptian tradition reflects the origins of architecture and art, like everything else in their traditions, to primeval times. In other words, everything must relate to the primordial scission. The antiquity of such knowledge is confirmed in the following points:

1. Plato wrote:

    "That the pictures and statues made ten thousand years ago, are in no one particular better or worse than what they now make."

    And taken in this limited sense — his remark indicates that the Egyptians were always bound by the same regulations, which ensured the consistent application, even to the latest times.
    Plato's statement is consistent with the evidence from the sculptures of the monuments erected after Egypt had long been a Roman province.

2. One process, peculiar to Egyptian temples, is growth by accretion, where successive kings often built additions to the same temple(s). A glance at some of these temples shows that the result is by no means in conflict with the laws of harmony. The added elements are interrelated and grow in scale (width and height) according to a certain rule of proportion connecting them to the original building. A good example is to be found at the huge complex of the great Karnak Temple. Although it was built over a span of more than 1,500 years, and features 6 pylons, it is still an imposing and homogeneous achievement that produced a harmonious plan of buildings covering about 7,550 ft (2,300 m) in perimeter.
    It is obvious that the overall plan pre-existed and that it was known to those who executed it.

3. Archeological findings show that these rules were put
into writing on rolls of papyrus or leather and carefully
kept in special archives in the great Egyptian temples.
This is explicitly stated in a number of texts from various periods dealing exclusively with architecture and
crafts, such as:

a. A passage from the stela of King Neferhotep (5,000
years ago) at Abtu (Abydos), describes his plan to seek
original information from the archives about the exact traditional form of the statue of Ausar (Osiris):

*The King spake to the nobles and companions, the
scribes of hieroglyphs: "My heart hath desired to see
the ancient writings of Atum; open ye for me for a great
investigation; let the neter [god] know concerning his
creation, and the neteru [gods/goddesses] concerning
their fashioning, their offerings and their oblations...
[let] me know the neter [god] in his form, that I may
fashion him as he was formerly, when they made the
[statues] in their council, in order to establish their
monuments upon earth.*

These earliest Egyptian records indicate that the forms
of the statues of neteru (gods/goddesses), and presumably also of other artistic and architectural features,
had the following characteristics:

- They were well defined.
- The definitions were transmitted by means
  of written specifications.
- The specifications were kept in archives.
- The archives existed in all official institu-
  tions, such as law courts, public works,
  cadastres, as well as in temples.
- High officials, as well as kings, had access
  to archives.
- The high officials were required to study
  and implement the specifications.

King Neferhotep's stela then describes the extent of the exact shape of the neter's (god's) statue — even the fingers:

The King proceeded to the library. He opened the rolls together with these companions. Lo, he found the rolls of the House of Ausar [Osiris], First of the Westerners, lord of Abtu [Abydos]. The King said to these companions: "My person hails my father Ausar [Osiris], First of the Westerners, lord of Abtu [Abydos] I will fashion [him, his limbs-his face, his fingers] according to that which my person has seen in the rolls [—] his [forms]".

b. Amenhotep, son of Hapu, who was an outstanding scholar and the architect for Amenhotep III (1405-1367 BCE), describes his early education:

"I was appointed to be an entry-level king's scribe; I was introduced into the divine book, I beheld the excellent things of Tehuti [Thoth]; I was equipped with their knowledge; I opened all their [passages]; one took counsel with me on all their matters."

c. Queen Hatshepsut, building the temple on Ta-Apet's (Thebes/Luxor) West Bank,

"... It was according to the ancient plan"

Senmut, the renowned architect of Queen Hatshepsut, wrote:

"I was a noble, to whom one harkened; moreover, I had access to all the writings of the nobles; there was nothing that I did not know of that which had happened since the beginning."

This was not idle talk, for Senmut inscribed on his stela an archaic text that had been out of fashion for a long time. Some of the writings are described as being on leather rolls, such as the records of Amun at Karnak during the New Kingdom, or the rolls of the library of the temple at Edfu.

d. From texts inscribed in the crypts of the temple of **Het-Heru** (Hathor) at Dendara we know that the temple was rebuilt during the Ptolemaic Era, and that it was planned according to an ancient document:

"The venerable foundation in Dendara was found in early writings, written on a leather roll in the time of the Servants of Heru (= the kings preceding Mena/Menes), at Men-Nefer [Memphis], in a casket, at the time of the lord of the Two Lands... Pepi."

☞ It is accordingly clear that the project of restoration during the Greco-Roman period was based on drawings dating back to Pepi's reign in the 6th Dynasty (2400 BCE), themselves claimed to be copies of predynastic documents (before 3000 BCE).

Homage to the Perfect

As explained earlier, the dynamics necessary for creation and its progression follow an asymmetrical division.

The wobble of the earth about its own axis (responsible for the precession of the equinoxes) is a result of this natural, invariable law. The generative power behind the created universe provokes the fundamental asymmetry reflected in shifts of the axes themselves.

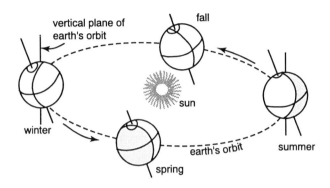

The axes of most of the Egyptian monumental buildings, especially temples, are curved. This is not an error, but rather a conscious act. Every line in the Universe, that is nothing but Movement, will be curved.

Although the ancient Egyptians were usually meticulous, they have always intentionally left out something (which may appear as an error) in graphic design, sculpture, painting, texts, and buildings.

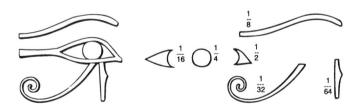

In Egypt, the sections of the eye are the glyphs for the fractions $^1/_2$ to $^1/_{64}$. The parts total $^{63}/_{64}$. The sum of successive division will always fall short of unity except at infinity, which is perfectly consonant with Egyptian thought: only the Absolute is One.

The Harmonic Design Parameters

Harmonic design in ancient Egyptian architecture was achieved through a unification of two systems:

- arithmetic (significant numbers).

- graphic (square, rectangles, and a few triangles).

The union of the two systems reflects the relationship of the parts to the whole, which is the essence of harmonic design.

This union of arithmetic and graphic design follows the elements described below.

1 - The Active Axes

An axis is an imaginary and ideal line about which a moving body revolves. In geometry, an axis is equally imaginary — a line without thickness.

The Egyptian temple was regarded as an organic, living unity. It is in constant motion; its intricate alignments, and its multiple asymmetries, make it oscillate about its axes.

This movement takes place within a rhythm given by the "module", or the particular coefficient of the thing or idea to be defined.

Ancient Egyptian architectural design is conspicuous for its strong apparent symmetry around a longitudinal axis. This is the result of the ancient Egyptian knowledge of cosmic laws. The Egyptian designer reflected such slight cosmic asymmetry, by ensuring that elements on either side of the axis are not exactly identical to one another. While most of them are balanced, elements are not symmetrical.

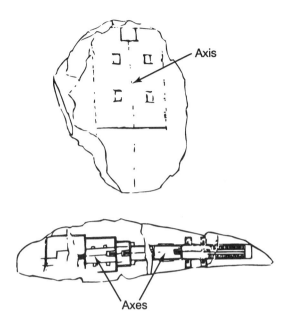

Two examples of axes defined on ancient Egyptian drawings.

The axis line can be found in a few recovered architectural drawings or sketches on papyri and tablets from various periods. They were, presumably, workmen's notations, and in spite of their practical purpose, they still feature the axis line drawn in the same conventional way as in modern drawings.

In the buildings themselves, the axis is marked by an engraved line on the stones of the upper course of a foundation slab, such as the case at Luxor Temple.

2 - Significant Points (Along the Axis)

Significant points were determined along the design axis. These points mark the intersection with transverse axes, the alignment of a central doorway, the position of an altar, the center of the sanctuary, etc. These significant points follow a precise arithmetic progression. In many of the best plans, these significant points are at harmonic distances from one another, and their distances from one end to the other express the figures of the Summation (so-called *Fibonacci*) Series, 3, 5, 8, 13, 21, 34, 55, 89, 144, 233, 377, 610, . . . The harmonic analysis shows a series of significant points readable from both ends, i.e. if inverted, a system of significant points would also correspond to the Series with the reference point starting at the opposite end of the plan.

High numbers of the Summation Series were crystallized in the Egyptian monuments ever since the Old Kingdom. The design of the pyramid temple of **Khafra** (Chephren) reaches the figure of 233 cubits in its total length, as measured from the pyramid, with a complete series of TEN significant points. The Karnak Temple follows the Summation Series' figures up to 610 cubits, i.e. TWELVE significant points. [See diagrams of both temples in Knot 13.]

3 - The Telescopic Triangles

The typical Egyptian temple plan increases in width and height from the sanctuary towards the front. This over-all delimitation was based upon a "telescopic system" of design since the Old Kingdom. The increase in width was accomplished by the use of consecutive 1:2, 1:4, and 1:8 triangles from one or more significant point(s).

[See diagram of Karnak Temple (partial) on the opposite page.]

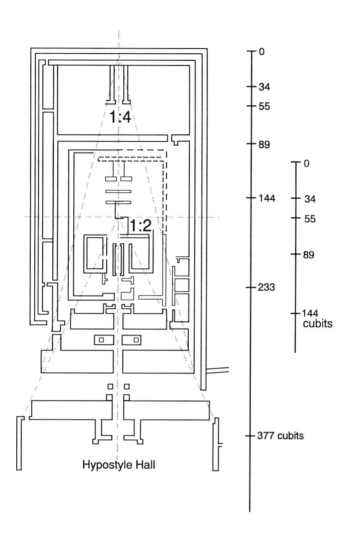

Typical Telescopic Triangles in Ancient Egyptian Design

4 - The Rectangular Perimeters

The general horizontal and vertical outlines are basically rectangular in shape, for the overall plan as well as its constituent parts.
Different configurations were used, such as:

• A simple square, such as the pyramid in the valley portal of Khafra (Chephren) Temple in Giza.

• A double square or 1:2 rectangle, such as the Zoser Complex at Saqqara, the inner enclosure at Karnak, and the festival hall of Tuthomosis III.

• The Neb (Golden) Rectangle — numerous examples.

• Root Rectangles — numerous examples.

5 - The Vertical Plane

Harmonic proportion was applied by the ancient Egyptians in all three dimensions, such as:

• The pyramids (square bases and triangle volume).

• The striking case of the King's Room in Khufu (Cheops) Pyramid, which affords exact relations for the great diagonal in space with respect to the dimension of the side. [See diagram on page 139.]

• Pylons. [See diagram on pages 162-3.]

• Doorways/portals/gates. [See diagram on pages 164-5.]

• Vertical heights seem to have followed the same proportional increase as horizontal widths, as additions were made to the front of monuments — an aspect characteristic of the Egyptian temples.

Design and Construction Plans

The Egyptian architecture was like our modern concept of a design-built system. It was a practical application, and the architect was the master builder.

The basic features of architects' plans in ancient Egypt were drawn on papyri. Only a few examples have survived. There are a number of architectural sketches that were executed on limestone fragments.

Samples of such drawings and sketches are:

1.   A papyrus that was found in Zoser's Pyramid Complex (3rd Dynasty) at Saqqara. The papyrus shows the definition of the curve of a roof, by a system of coordinates. The vertical lines are shown placed at equal distances from one another, and the numbers  indicating their length from an unmarked horizontal level define the coordinates of a number of points on the curve. This is proof that the Egyptians had a very exact idea of graphic representation at least 5,000 years ago.

2.   The papyrus in the Museum at Turin contains a projected design for the tomb of Ramses IV. There are differences in proportion between the design and the tomb as we know it today, which indicates that the design

was created prior to the excavation of the tomb and confirms that it represents a project and not a survey.

The plan shows, among other things, the contours of the excavation indicated by double strokes. The dimensions of each room (length, width and height) are shown clearly. Details (such as doors) are sketched on the plan in reduced elevation.

It is quite likely that this general plan was complimented by more detailed working diagrams, which is also the case in present-day construction projects.

3. A limestone fragment, more than 30" (76cm) long. This project for the tomb of Ramses IX is very similar to that shown on the Turin Papyrus.

4. A papyrus with a grid, dating from the New Kingdom [see next page] shows a remarkable design for a shrine. It shows that the Egyptians knew how to represent an object from several angles. The two elevations reveal a number of interior features, as in a transparency, and also display the part of sections. It shows how exact these designs could be.

5. There are some drawings with squared grids of the front and side elevations of naoi, capitals, and statues identical to those used for drawings of figures and scenes [see opposite page]. Squared grids were also used on walls or on blocks that were to be carved into statues. Human figures, animals, sphinxes, and even capitals and naoi, were designed, copied, or enlarged from books of models by means of grids.

Squaring on a grid was often used for wall decorations. Remains of such grids can still frequently be seen on the walls of tombs and temples.

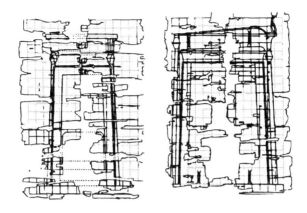

Front and side elevations of a wooden shrine, drawn on squared papyrus.

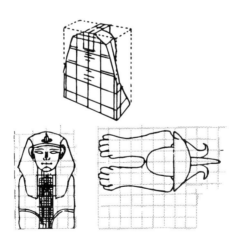

Knot 12

Temple, The Divine Energy Generator

The Function/Objective of The Temple

The Egyptian temple was a machine for maintaining and developing divine energy. Understanding this function helps us to regard Egyptian art as something vital and alive. Therefore, we must forego viewing the temple as an interplay of forms against a vague historical, archeological presentation. Instead, we must try to see it as the relationship between form and function and constructional techniques.

The temple is the link, the proportional mean, between the Macrocosmos (world) and Microcosmos (man). It was a stage on which meetings were enacted between the **neter** (god) and the king, as a representative of the people. It was the place in which the cosmic energy, **neter** (god) came to dwell and radiate its energy to the land and people.

As described in various ancient Egyptian texts, the temple or pylon is:

...as the pillars of heaven, [a temple] like the heavens, abiding upon their four pillars ... shining like the horizon of heaven ... a place of rest for the lord of neteru [gods], made like his throne that is in heaven ...like Ra when he rises in the horizon ... like Atum's great house of heaven".

Only after the Egyptian **neteru** (gods) had examined the temple destined for them, did they come and dwell there.

'When the great winged scarab rises from the primordial ocean and sails through the heavens in the guise of Heru [Horus] . . .he stops in the heaven before this temple and his heart is filled with joy as he look at it. Then he becomes one with his image, in his favorite place . . .. he is satisfied with the monument that the king . . . has erected for him.'

The harmonious power of the temple plans, the images engraved on the walls, and the forms of worship — all led to the same goal; a goal that was both spiritual, as it involved setting superhuman forces in motion, and practical, in that the final awaited result was the maintenance of the country's prosperity.

The Dynamic Walls (Bas-Relief)

The walls of the Egyptian temple were covered with animated images — including hieroglyphs — to facilitate the communication between the above and the below.

The ancient Egyptian framework was usually a square, representing the manifested world (squaring of the circle). Additionally, the square grid itself had the symbolic meaning of the manifested world, which also made it easy to construct the root rectangles of 2, 3, and 5, on/by the square(s) background.

The corners of squares and root rectangles were defined by notches along the perimeter, or carefully defined by incised lines.

Following are a few examples of the generative dynamic design layout:

1. A simple theme in root-two is exhibited in the figure below of the **netert** (goddess) Nut, the personification of the sky as matrix of all.

The spaces between the bars on either side of the figure were filled with hieroglyphic writing [removed here in order to show the geometric outlines].

- ABCD is a square.

- The diagonal BD = Ö2

- Point E was determined so that BE = BD = Ö2

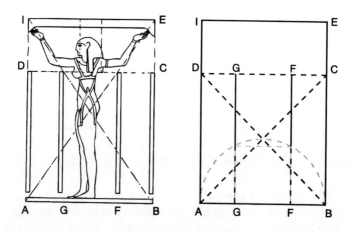

- Lines GG and FF were located based on the principle of inscribing a square into a half circle.

- The center of action is the hip joint of Nut.

2. Here we have a square that is defined by bars cut into the stone at the top and bottom of the composition. The area is dynamically divided for a pictorial composition. The plan of this arrangement is depicted below.

   - ABCD is a square.

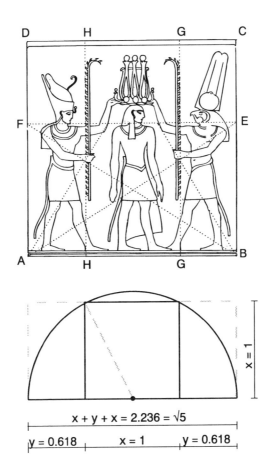

$$x + y + x = 2.236 = \sqrt{5}$$

$y = 0.618$ $x = 1$ $y = 0.618$

- A root-five rectangle was used in the center of a square, to determine the vertical lines GG and HH.

- The horizontal line EF forms a 5:8 rectangle ABEF.

3. The Egyptian bas-relief composition [opposite page] shows that its designer proportioned the picture, as well as the groups of hieroglyphs, by the application of whirling square rectangles to a square. The outlines of the major square are carefully incised into the stone by four bars, two of which have slight pointed projections on either end.

The following are just a few highlights of the design layout:

    - ABCD is a square.

    - A root-five rectangle was used in the center of a square, to determine the vertical lines at points G and H.

    - The horizontal line EF forms a 5:8 rectangle ABEF.

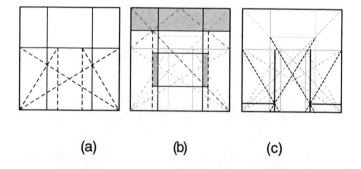

       (a)   (b)   (c)

    - The general construction plan was that of figure *(a)* above.

    - Spacing for the grouping of the hieroglyphic writing is in figure *(b)* above.

    - Spacing for additional elements of the design is shown in figure *(c)* above.

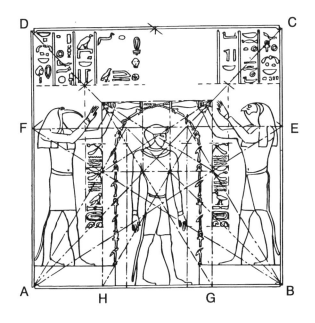

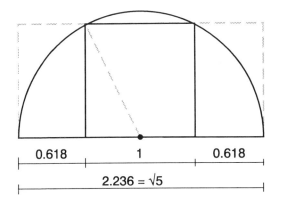

Practically all figures on the walls are in profile form, indicative of action and interaction between the various symbolic figures. A wide variety of actions in the forms are evident; a few of which are shown herein:

1. The immobile figure, a still profile, where the vertical axis passes through the ear (inner ear, equilibrium), hip joint, and ends in the heel of the foot.

2. The same as #1, except that both shoulders are shown, with a front view of the chest, indicative of restricted action.

3. Same as #2, except that one foot is positioned slightly ahead of the other — the beginning of movement.

4. The figure is in motion (the normal stride), when the axis of movement passes from the ear (balance) to the hip joint, and ends at the ball of the rear foot. It is on the ball of the foot that one places one's weight in order to move forward.

5. The running figure (the long stride), as shown on this original ancient Egyptian grid of the Bird Catcher, reminiscent of Papageno, in Mozart's Masonic Opera, *The Magic Flute*.

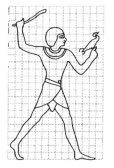

6. The action of working together.

7. Sitting broad-shouldered, in an active mode.

9. Leaning.

8. Kneeling and leaning.

10. The dancing girl, a four-step animated motion.

Let Energy Flow

In order to maintain the unity of the temple, its components must be connected so that the cosmic energy can flow
through unimpeded.

The unity of the components of the temple must be like
the components of the human body. The walls of a temple
consist of blocks and corners, and such components (blocks)
must be connected together in a way that allows the flow of
divine energy, just like the parts of the human being. It is
incorrect to merely think that a connection between two com-
ponents/parts are only to ensure the structural stability of
the part(s) and the whole building.

We can take clues from the human body (the house of
the soul) when reviewing the Egyptian temple (the house of
cosmic soul/energy/**neter**). The human body is connected
with muscles, ...etc., but veins and nerves are not interrupted
at the bone joints of the skeleton. The living ancient Egyptian temple was designed likewise. Bas-reliefs of all sizes, as

well as the hieroglyphic symbols, span two adjoining blocks
with total perfection. The intent is very clear — to bridge
over the joint between adjacent blocks (next to each other,
or on top of each other).

The blocks themselves were joined together in some type
of nerve/energy system. A continuation of energy flow required special interlocking patterns. The practice of joining
blocks together prevailed in every Egyptian temple throughout the known history of ancient Egypt. Here are a few examples of joining applications:

1. Cutting into each block of stone, a superficial, 1 inch
    (2cm) deep, dovetail-type notch that linked the stone to
    the adjacent stone. These mortices link one block to an-
    other — a kind of nervous or arterial system running
    throughout the whole of the temple. [See illustration on
    opposite page.]
    No binding material has ever been found in these shal-
    low dovetail notches. There is no architectural or struc-
    tural importance, whatsoever, for such notches, with or
    without wooden tenons.

2. There are frequent, intentional, well-defined, rectangu-
    lar, neat, man-made hammer marks on top of the blocks.
    Again, these have no structural value whatsoever. [See
    illustration on opposite page.]

3. Columns made of single, circular blocks have their sec-
    tions connected with a well-defined circle of neat ham-
    mer marks. Again, these have no structural value what-
    soever. [See illustration on opposite page.]

4. Columns built of semi-circular blocks (expressing dual-
    ity) are found to have a superficial, 1" (2cm) deep, dove-
    tail-type notch between the two semi-circular blocks.
    Again, these notches are architecturally and structur-
    ally meaningless. [See illustration on opposite page.]

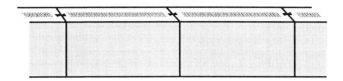

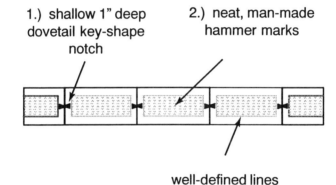

1.) shallow 1" deep
dovetail key-shape
notch

2.) neat, man-made
hammer marks

well-defined lines

well-defined lines

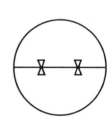

3.) single block column   4.) dual block column

Western Ta-Apet (Thebes/Luxor)

5.   Paving blocks in and around ancient Egyptian monuments are set in mosaic style, in order to avoid pointed corners and continuous crack lines, such as the huge paving blocks around the pyramids of Giza. One can clearly see these very durable, perfectly fitted, square-angled blocks, which are several yards (meters) in length.

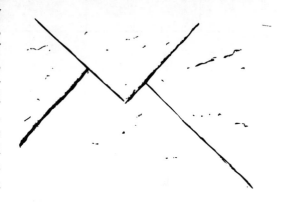

Ancient Egyptians, throughout history, avoided the simple abrupt interlocking joints. Creating uninterrupted continuous corners allowed the energies to flow unimpeded.

Knot 13

Harmonic Analysis of Ancient Egyptian Works

General

The ancient Egyptians manifested their knowledge in harmonic proportion, long before its pre-dynastic era, and continuing throughout its dynastic history. The selected diagrams shown on the next pages are just a few examples, spread along Egypt's long-known history. Please note:

1 - The diagrams are based on measurements by various and independent sources [see page 181 for each specific reference].

2 - In order not to overwhelm the reader with crowded drawings, columns and many details of the ancient Egyptian monuments are not shown on the following diagrams. Simpler layout drawings will make it easier for the reader to see the consistent application of harmonic proportion in the Egyptian works.

3 - In some cases, distances shown in these diagrams were converted into Egyptian cubits, so that the ancient Egyptian knowledge and consistent use of the Summation (so called *Fibonacci*) Series becomes very clear.

4 - Of the example buildings used in this chapter (and the entire book), none of them have been touched during foreign rule, so there is not the slightest doubt that Egyptians had this knowledge long before any foreigners ever invaded Egypt.

Pre-Dynastic Era (5000-2575 BCE)

Because of the remote age of the pre-dynastic era, only mastaba-type tombs survived, in the remote areas of Egypt. The superstructure of the mastaba tombs, even during the pre-dynastic era, followed harmonic proportions, as evident in tombs in the Abtu(Abydos), Men-Nefer (Memphis), and Giza areas.

A large number of Egyptian mastabas were documented by Aug. Mariette (*General catalogue of the monuments of Abydos*, Paris 1880). Mariette found about 800 of them during his excavations at Abtu (Abydos).

Most of the simplest tombs conformed to the 5:8 Neb (Golden) rectangle.

Several tombs were composed of a combination of a square and a 5:8 Neb (Golden) rectangle.

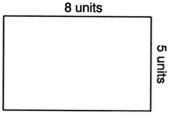

8 units

5 units

To have hundreds of tombs throughout the country with such harmonic proportion shows that it was common knowledge, even at that early age.

• • •

Since temples require restoration every few decades/centuries, we find that every temple in Egypt, includes references that they were built in pre-dynastic times. As such, temples from various dynastic eras are generally restorations of pre-dynastic works.

Old Kingdom (2575-2150 BCE)

Mastaba Tombs

In order to show that harmonic proportion was common knowledge, here are a few examples of mastaba-type tombs in Giza. The rectangular superstructures are oriented north-south, and show harmonic designs, as shown below.

- Mastaba Tomb 6 (Giza)

The constructional diagram consists of a square and a 5:8 Neb (Golden) rectangle.

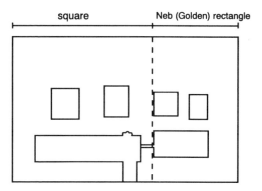

Most other tombs are a simple 5:8 Neb (Golden) rectangle, as per the indicated measurements:

- Mastaba Tomb 86 (Giza): 12.6' (3.85m) x 20.1' (6.17m)

- Mastaba Tomb 87 (Giza): 19.1' (5.82m) x 31.2' (9.52m)

- Mastaba Tomb 105 (Giza): 9.7' (2.95m) x 15.6' (4.75m)

Old Kingdom (cont.)

Khufu (Cheops) Pyramid's Granite Room

Khufu's pyramid is located in Giza, and was built during his reign (2551-2528 BCE).
The floor plan of the room is a double square (2 x 1 rectangle), 20 x 10 Egyptian cubits (34'-4" x 17'-2", 10.5 x 5.2m).

The double square, divided by a single diagonal CA, forms two right triangles, each having a base of 1 and a height of 2. The diagonal CA is equal to the square root of 5 (2.236), i.e. 22.36 cubits in actual length.

The height of the room is designed to be one half the length of the floor diagonal CA, i.e. $\sqrt{5}/2$, which is 11.18 cubits (19'-2" or 5.8m) in actual length.

This choice of CD, as the height of the room, will make the diagonal DB (in the triangle DCB) equal to 15 cubits. The result is that the three sides of the triangle ABD are in relation of 3:4:5.

The harmonic proportion of this room shows the intimate relationship between 1:2:3:4:5, and demonstrates the relationship in the divine harmonic proportion *(sacred geometry)* between process and structure. It also shows that the right-angle triangle principle (so-called *Pythagoras*) was practiced in the Egyptian design regularly, 2,000 years before Pythagoras walked this earth.

• • •

Complete analysis of the interior and exterior of masonry pyramids in Egypt is detailed in *Pyramid Handbook*, by Moustafa Gadalla, ISBN 0-9652509-4-6.

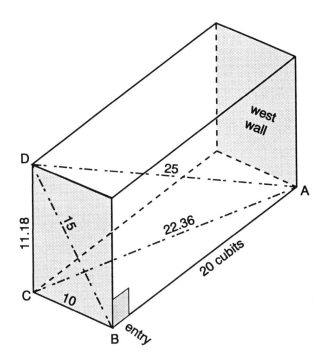

Granite Room of Khufu's Pyramid

Old Kingdom (cont.)

Pyramid Temple of Khafra

This temple was built during Khafra's (Chephren) reign (2520-2494 BCE), and is located in Giza next to his pyramid. Points of interesting harmonic proportion in this massive, yet very exact structure include:

1 - The almost symmetrical plan. [See pages 112-4.]

2 - It consists of two squares connected by a 5:8 Neb (Golden) rectangle.

3 - All significant points [explained on page 116] are clearly connected, even to the corners of the massive piers.

4 - The significant points along the longitudinal axis correspond to the numbers of the Summation (so-called *Fibonacci*) Series [3, 5, 8, 13, 21, 34, 55, **89**, 144, **233**, 377, 610,...]. The total length to the pyramid is **233** cubits, while the width is **89** cubits, two figures that closely correspond to the constructional diagram [see opposite page] $89 \times 2 + \frac{5}{8} \times 89 = 233 \frac{5}{8}$ cubits.
The intermediate numbers mark the doorways or the alignment of the stepped plan in the front hall.

• • •

Complete analysis of the interior and exterior of masonry pyramids in Egypt is detailed in *Pyramid Handbook*, by Moustafa Gadalla, ISBN 0-9652509-4-6.

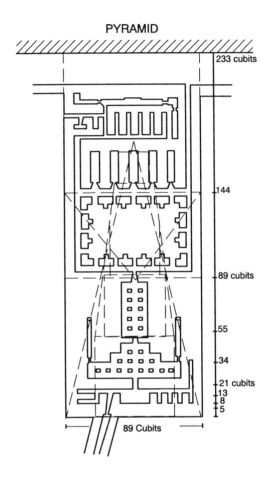

PYRAMID

233 cubits

144

89 cubits

55

34

21 cubits
13
8
5

89 Cubits

← square
← Neb (Golden) Rectangle
← square

Pyramid Temple of Khafra

Old Kingdom (cont.)

Menkaura's (Mycerinus) Pyramid

This is the last masonry pyramid built during the Pyramid Age that started with Zoser (2630-2611 BCE).

This pyramid is the smallest and youngest of the three pyramids on the Giza Plateau. It was built by Menkaura (2494-2472 BCE), and has the following interesting harmonic design characteristics:

1 - The base is a perfect square with four triangular-shaped surfaces in space.

2 - Its cross section is very nearly a 5:8 triangle, representing the Neb (Golden) triangle.

3 - The ratio of the height to half the diagonal is 8:9 (the perfect musical tone).

Menkaura's pyramid represents the perfect harmony for sight and sound.

This pyramid signified the end of the Pyramid Age.

•   •   •

Complete analysis of the interior and exterior of masonry pyramids in Egypt is detailed in *Pyramid Handbook*, by Moustafa Gadalla, ISBN 0-9652509-4-6.

Base: 356' square (108m)
[error from true north = 14"]
Height: 218' (67m)
Mass: 0.6 million tons
Slope: (face to base) 51° 20' 25" (5/4)
         (edge to base) 51° 29' 53" (8/9)

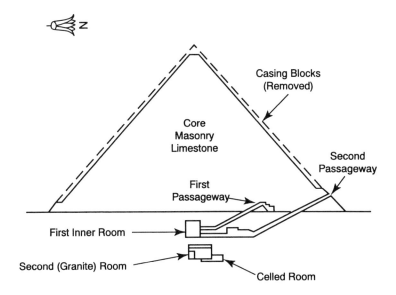

Menkaura's Pyramid

Middle Kingdom (2040-1783 BCE)

Peripteral Chapel Of Sen-usert (Sesostris) I

The pavilion of Sen-usert I (1971-1926 BCE), at the Karnak Temple Complex, incorporates geodesic knowledge in its design, and it also provides a wealth of geodesic information on its walls. It has a list of all the provinces of Egypt with their respective land surface areas, proving that actual surveys were made. Major towns are listed, the total length of Egypt is given, and the normal height of the Nile flood at three principal points along the length of the river is noted. Much additional useful information is also provided on these walls.

The constructional diagram is a square, flanked by a 5:8 Neb (Golden) rectangle on each side, delimiting the length of both stairways.

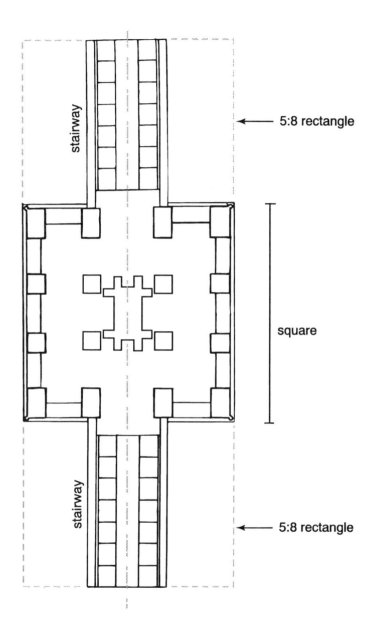

stairway

5:8 rectangle

square

stairway

5:8 rectangle

Peripteral Chapel of Sen-Usert

Middle Kingdom (cont.)

Tomb of Wahka

Wakha's rock-cut tomb was constructed ca. 1900 BCE at Qaw near Asyut, and is partly cut into the cliff. The layout is terraced, featuring a pillared portico, sloping causeway, stairway, courtyard, and superimposed columned porticos.

Points of interesting harmonic proportions include:

1 - The upper part of the complex, stretching on many levels, consists of squares connected by a scissors-like lattice of 5:8 **Neb** (Golden) triangles/rectangles.

2 - The complex, excluding the front stairway, is proportioned based on five numbers of the Summation (Fibonacci) Series.

This example shows that far away from the populated centers of **Men-Nefer** (Memphis) and **Ta-Apet** (Thebes), harmonic proportion was common knowledge, throughout the country.

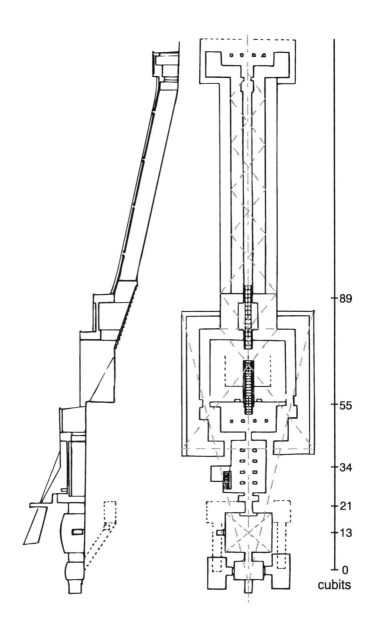

89

55

34

21

13

0
cubits

Tomb of Wahka

New Kingdom (1550-1070 BCE)

Karnak Temple Complex

The original sanctuary of the Karnak Complex at Ta-Apet (Thebes) was built during the Middle Kingdom.

This is the largest complex of temples in Egypt, where the temples, pylons, courts, columns and reliefs were continually added to, from the Middle to the Late Kingdom, i.e. for over 1500 years.

Although dating from various periods, the temples comply with the principles of harmonic design. This is important evidence to support the existence of archives where records of the projects were kept for reference.

This is a good example of a temple constructed by accretion through successive additions (always to the front), of larger and larger courtyards and pylons.

●   ●   ●

If we consider only the main axis (west-east) temple, we will find that more than one Summation (Fibonacci) Series [3, 5, 8, 13, 21, 34, 55, 89, 144, 233, 377, **610**, ...] of significant points shows the application of the comprehensive harmonic design, along three different scales. The greatest distance is **610** cubits, from the external rear to the axis of the triple shrine of Amun, Mut, and Khonsu, in the front courtyard.

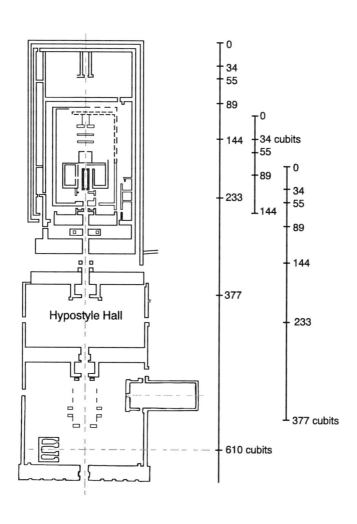

Karnak Temple
Main Axis (West-East)

𝓝ew 𝓚ingdom (cont.)

Ausar (Osiris) Temple

This well-preserved temple at **Abtu** (Abydos) has an unusual L-shaped plan. This work is dated to Seti I (1333-1304 BCE) and was completed by Ramses II (1304-1237 BCE).

Points of interesting harmonic proportion include:

1 - The harmonic design took into account the shift of the lateral part of the L-shape. The basic scheme is continuous throughout the main body and lateral part of the plan.
The temple outline plan consists of a square topped with three 5:8 **Neb** (Golden) rectangles and the rear lateral section is one 5:8 **Neb** (Golden) rectangle of the same width as the main portion.

2 - A series of significant points are determined in the main body, beginning at the rear wall of the sanctuaries. The distances coincide with the numbers of the Summation (so-called *Fibonacci*) Series [3,5,8,13,21,34,55,89,144, **233**, **377**, 610,...], up to **233** cubits, which determines the front alignment of the two enclosures in the forecourt.
It is noteworthy that the subsequent number of the series, **377**, determines the total length of the temple, if the lateral portion of the L-shape is stretched out to the axis of the outer gateway opening on to the lateral part.

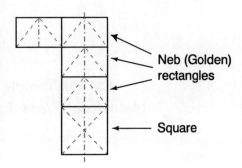

Neb (Golden) rectangles

Square

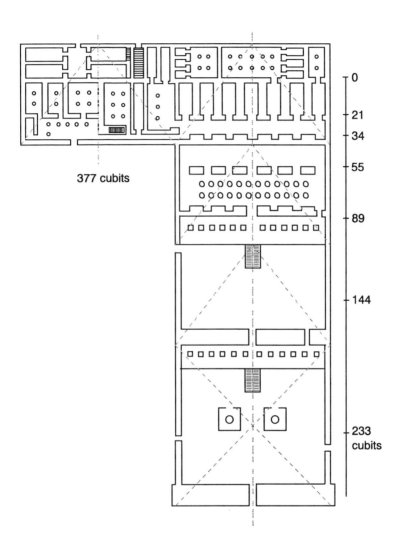

377 cubits

0
21
34
55
89
144
233
cubits

Ausar Temple

New Kingdom (cont.)

Tomb of Ramses IV

The tomb of King Ramses IV (1163-1156 BCE) in the Valley of Kings, at Ta-Apet (Thebes), has the following interesting harmonic features:

1 - The tomb *OPQR* contains a triple sarcophagus. The tomb itself was dimensioned on a projection of the geometry of this triple sarcophagus.

2 - The innermost sarcophagus *ABCD* is in the form of a double square — the holiest of sacred enclosures.

3 - The middle sarcophagus *EFGH* is in the form of a 5:8 Neb (Golden) rectangle.

4 - The outer sarcophagus *IJLM* has two 5:8 Neb (Golden) rectangles *IJKN* and *NKLM* each of which is equal to the middle sarcophagus *EFGH*.

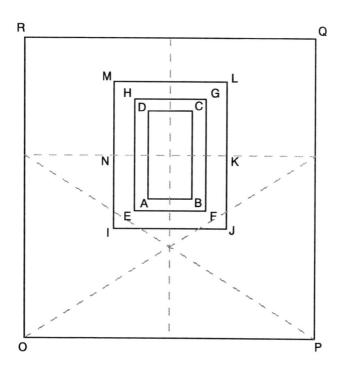

Tomb of Ramses IV

The Last Native Egyptian Pharaoh

Khnum Temple

This temple was erected by the last Egyptian Pharaoh, Nectanebo II (360-343 BCE) at Elephantine, and was enlarged during the Ptolemaic and Roman era. The temple shows that even at the end of Egypt's dynastic history, the general layout followed a well-defined harmonic scheme. The temple has points of interesting harmonic proportion, such as:

1 - Prior to the Ptolemaic era, the temple's width was established as **55** cubits at its rear. The length was extended during the reign of Egyptian Nectanebo II to **89** cubits, with 8 significant points corresponding to the numbers of the Summation (*Fibonacci*) Series.

   Then later during the Ptolemaic rule, the row of columns in the vestibule was built at the **89** cubit length so that the scheme of the harmonic diagram is a square **89** topped with a 5:8 **Neb** (Golden) rectangle.

   With the later additions of a rear enclosure, forecourt, and pylon, the total length amounts to **233** cubits, with an intermediate significant point evident at **144** cubits from the rear end to the alignment of the forecourt before its final arrangement.

2 - All the above critical distances such as **55**, **89**, **144**, and **233** are clearly numbers from the Summation (so-called *Fibonacci*) Series [3, 5, 8, 13, 21, 34, **55**, **89**, **144**, **233**, 377, 610, ...].

3 - This shows that temple construction in ancient Egypt, even under foreign rule, was based on purely ancient Egyptian design criteria, as is obvious in the earlier works in ancient Egypt, and was learned subsequently by these invaders.

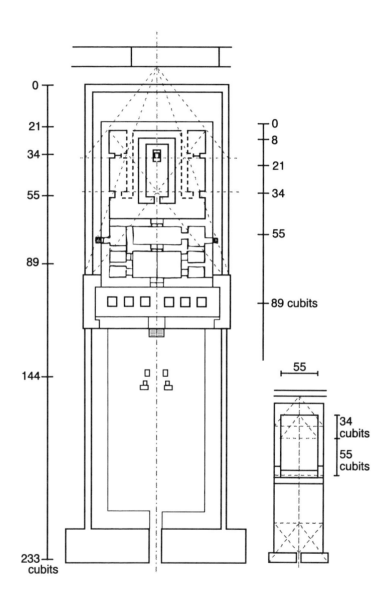

Khnum Temple

Restorations During Greco-Roman Period

(332 BCE - 395 CE)

Several Ancient Egyptian temples were restored during the Greco-Roman period. The restored temples show consistent compliance with the Egyptian canon of proportion that has been utilized for the prior several thousand years.

A clear example comes from texts inscribed in the crypts of the temple of **Het-Heru** (Hathor) at Dendara that was rebuilt during the Ptolemaic Era, based on drawings dating back to King Pepi of the 6th Dynasty (2400 BCE). The drawings themselves are copies of pre-dynastic documents.

The text reads:

"The venerable foundation in Dendera was found in early writings, written on a leather roll in the time of the Servants of Heru (= the kings preceding Mena/Menes), at Men-Nefer [Memphis], in a casket, at the time of the lord of the Two Lands... Pepi."

It is evident that restoration work done during the Greco-Roman period was done according to ancient Egyptian knowledge.

Miscellaneous Items

General

Harmonic design was not restricted to the large ancient Egyptian architectural monuments, but was used in the smaller structures and elements such as capitals and stelae, as well as in graphic compositions and statuary, which are all parts of the whole — the temple.

The pectorals and other magic amulets found on mummified Egyptians have been geometrically analyzed. They all show various configurations of harmonic proportion, which demonstrates the unity of Egyptian sacred geometry from the largest to the smallest sacred object.

We shall present a few examples of smaller (relatively speaking) items, such as:

- Capitals of Columns

- Stelae

- Pylons

- Doorways/Gateways

Miscellaneous Items (cont.)

Capitals of Columns

The design of capitals in ancient Egypt was based on 1:2, 1:4, and 5:8 Neb (Golden) triangles. The following are three types of Egyptian-designed capitals:

1 - The **papyriform** capital — from Ramses III Commemorative Temple (Medinat Habu), western Ta-Apet (Luxor) — the diameter of the capital is twice that of the shaft or abacus. A 5:8 Neb (Golden) triangle defines the proportions between the widest edge of the corolla, acting as a base, and the third of the five binding rings.

2 - The **lotiform** or papyriform bud capital — Karnak Temple (ca. 1335 BCE) — the constructional diagram for the outline features a square, derived proportionally from the diameter of the shaft by means of a 5:8 Neb (Golden) triangle and giving the height of the trapezoidal cross section of the bud. The widths at the top and bottom of the bud are determined by two 5:8 triangles. It is noteworthy that the decoration of the five rings and the stylized vertical stems beneath have a square outline.

3 - The peculiar inverted **campaniform** capital of the tent-pole column, in the festival hall of Tuthomosis III (1490-1436 BCE) at Karnak, has its height determined by the height of the 5:8 triangle whose base equals the largest diameter of the corolla.

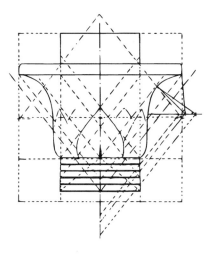

1. Papyriform capital from Medinat Habu

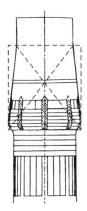

3. Campaniform capital in festival hall of Tuthomosis III at Karnak Temples

2. Lotiform or papyriform bud capital at Karnak Temples

Miscellaneous Items (cont.)

Stelae

Egyptian stelae from different eras were designed according to well-defined harmonic proportions. Examples of the internal panel configurations are:

1. Stela of King Watchi at Abtu **(Abydos)**, 1st Dynasty (ca. 3100 BCE)

A square topped with a 5:8 Neb (Golden) triangle.

2. Stela 20088 at Cairo Museum, Middle Kingdom (2040-1783 BCE)

Twin squares.

3. Stela 20255 at Cairo Museum, Middle Kingdom.

Twin 5:8 Neb (Golden) rectangles.

1. Stela of King Watchi

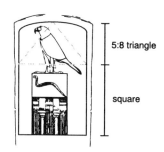

5:8 triangle

square

2. Stela 20088

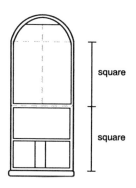

square

square

3. Stela 20255

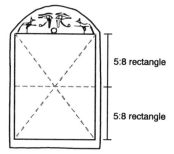

5:8 rectangle

5:8 rectangle

Miscellaneous Items (cont.)

Pylons

Pylons are a permanent feature of Egyptian temples. An example of the harmonic proportion of an Egyptian pylon is located at the Temple of Khonsu (ca. 1330 BCE) at the Karnak Temple Complex. The unique harmonic proportion of this 19th Dynasty pylon was noted in *The description of Egypt*, [Part III, page 57], written during Napoleon's time.

The whole width is divided into three parts: M + m + M. The portal takes up the middle part of the width, and there are pylon towers arising on both sides of the portal.

Whole width	= B
Whole height	= H
Width of the Pylon-Tower	= M
Width of the portal/gate	= m
Opening of the gate, height	= h
Opening of the gate, width	= b

Points of interest in the harmonic proportion are:

1 -   The ratio of total width to total height (B/H) = 1.618. That means that the pylon forms a vertical Neb (Golden) rectangle.

2 -   M/m = 1.618, i.e. the ratio of the width of the pylon to the width of the portal is the Neb (Golden) proportion.

3 -   Each pylon-tower is a golden rectangle in the vertical plane. (H/M = 1.618)

4 -   The relationships between B, H, M, and m are:
$$B \times 0.618 = H$$
$$B \times 0.618^2 = M$$
$$B \times 0.618^3 = m$$

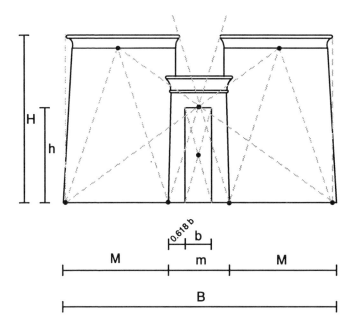

Temple of Khonsu

Miscellaneous Items (cont.)

Doorways/Gateways

In ancient Egypt, doorways were built with or without a pylon on each side.

A few examples from different periods show that the simple design of Egyptian doorways conforms to a harmonic analysis. The relationships between the openings and the doorjambs were harmonically proportioned. The height of the aperture and the full height, were also harmonically designed.

Points of interesting harmonic proportions are:

1 - The overall outline in the vertical plane is the double-square, 1:2 ratio.

2 - The opening width is based on a square inscribed within a semi-circle, the typical ancient Egyptian way of proportioning a root-five rectangle.
Thus, the thickness of the doorjamb is 0.618 the width of the opening.

3 - The width of the opening (b) = h x 1/2 x 0.618.

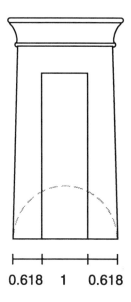

0.618   1   0.618

This is the Gateway to Heaven,

for those who can see/hear

The Visual Music.

Glossary - General

abacus - a slab that forms the uppermost member or division of the capital of a column.

amulet - a charm or ornament containing special powers or symbolic representation.

BCE - Before Common Era. Also noted in other references as BC.

CE - Common Era. Also noted in other references as AD.

Circle Index - designates the ratio of the circumference of a circle to its diameter, and is equal to $^{22}/_7$, or 3.1415927.

corolla - the inner petals of a flower.

cubit - The ancient Egyptian unit of linear measurement, which is symbolized by the distance between the elbow and the tip of the middle finger of the extended hand.
one cubit   = 1.72' (0.5236m)

Heb-Sed - ancient festival associated with the rejuvenation of the spiritual and physical powers of the Pharaoh.

Heru - Heru is the falcon-deity, who is identified with the king during his lifetime. He is the son of Ausar(*Osiris*) and Auset(*Isis*). His centers are located in many places, e.g. Behdet in the Delta, and Edfu in Upper Egypt.

Het-Heru - Het-Heru is the provider of spiritual nourishment, pleasure, music, love, and dance. She is the consort of Heru(*Horus*). Her main temple was at Dendara. The Greeks associated her with *Aphrodite*.

mastaba - *Mastaba* is the Arabic word for *bench*; a mud-brick, above-ground structure. Below the mastaba are the burial chambers of the deceased.

The tombs consisted of subterrranean burial chambers with large, low, rectangular, mud-brick superstructures. The subterranean parts contained the burial chambers, which were surrounded by many other chambers and storage rooms for the less important funerary goods. The burial chamber was a narrow chamber hewn out of the rock, to which a shaft leads down from the roof of the mastaba.

The superstructures were rectangular, low in proportion to their lengths, and with convex roofs. They varied in size from 24 sq. yds. (20 sq. m) to an area of more than ¼ acre.

Neb (Golden) Proportion - is the *"key to the structure of the cosmos"*. If an approximation must be made, its value is 1.6180339-----.

Neter/Netert - Personification of divine principle. (incorrectly translated as *god/goddess*).

papyrus - Papyrus is a plant that is used to make a writing surface that is also called *papyrus*, meaning *paper*.

pectoral - coming from the breast or heart as the seat of emotion; situated in or on the chest.

perfect solid - a solid figure composed of plane faces, each of whose faces is identical and is an equilateral planar form, e.g., triangle, square or pentagon.

phi - (φ), *see* Neb (Golden) Proportion.

pi - (π), *see* Circle Index.

polyhedron - see *perfect solid*.

pylon - a towering structure flanking a temple's gateway. [See illustration on page 163.]

sacred geometry - The process by which all figures are to be drawn or created by using only a straight line (not even a ruler) and a compass, i.e. without measurement (dependent on proportion only).

segment - A geometric shape bound by a cord and an arc of a circle.

Seshat - netert (goddess) of writing/books and Lady of Builders. [See page 51.]

slope (common definition) - the amount or degree of the deviation from the horizontal or vertical in an inclined surface. The ratio of the vertical difference divided by the horizontal difference.

slope (in ancient Egypt) - For the ancient Egyptians, the slope was the length required for half the base when the height was equal to 1 (one cubit).

stele (plural: stelae) - stone or wooden slab or column decorated with commemorative inscriptions.

Tehuti - Neter(god) of wisdom and intellect. It was Tehuti, who uttered the words that created the world, as commanded by Ra. He was the messenger of the neteru(gods), of writing, of language, of knowledge.

Thoth - See Tehuti (the Egyptian name).

vertex - the point opposite to and farthest from the base in a figure; a point that terminates a line or curve or comprises the intersection of two or more lines.

Glossary - Musical

beat - A constant pulsation. It acts as a ruler by which we can measure time.

chord - the string of a musical instrument. A combination of three or more tones sounded together in harmony.

chromatic - chroma = color. A scale in which the intervals between the notes are all semitones.

diapason - the entire compass of musical tones. A burst of harmonious sound.

diatonic - A scale consisting of 5 whole tones and 2 semitones (from the 3rd to the 4th, and from the 7th to the octave).

enharmonic - Designating a ¼ step/note.

fret - narrow, lateral ridges fixed across the finger board of a guitar, etc., to regulate the fingering.

halftone - *see* semitone.

Intervals Table -

Interval	Ratio	Largest number
unison	1:1	1
octave	2:1	2
fifth	3:2	3
fourth	4:3	4
major third	5:4	5
major sixth	5:3	5
minor third	6:5	6
minor sixth	8:5	8
whole-tone	9:8	9
semi-tone	256:245	256

measure - the notes or rests or both contained between two vertical lines on the staff, subdividing a part of a composition into equal groups of beats.

notes - In Western musical terms, the letters A to G are used to designate notes.

pitch - The position of a tone in a musical scale, determined by the frequency of vibration, and measured by cycles per second.

scales - Any series of tones arranged in a step-by-step rising or falling of pitch. Conventional music relies on the use of scales, which consist of a given pattern of intervals (the differences of pitch between notes). These intervals are described in terms of tones, semitones, and smaller.
The most common scales are: diatonic, chromatic, and enharmonic.

semitone - the intervals between B and C, and between E and F. (*also see* **Tone**).

stanza - a group of lines of verse forming one of the divisions of a poem or song. It typically has a regular pattern in the number of lines and the arrangement of meter and rhyme.

timber - the color of the sound invoked. Playing the same note on both the guitar and piano, timber defines/differentiates one sound from the other.

tone - The combination of pitch, intensity (loudness) and quality (timber). The interval between each of the notes is a tone, except between B and C, and between E and F, where the interval is a semitone in each case.

Selected Bibliography

Assmann, J. *Agyptische Hymnen Und Gebete* (Leiden Papyrus p. 312-321), Zürich/Münich, 1975.

Badawy, Alexander. *Ancient Egyptian Architectural Design.* Los Angeles, CA, USA, 1965.

Brophy, Brigid. *Mozart The Dramatist.* New York, 1988.

Chace, Arnold Buffum. *The Rhind Mathematical Papyrus.* Ohio, USA, 1929.

Choisy, Auguste. *Historie de L'Architecture, I.* Paris, France, 1899.

DeCenival, Jean-Louis. *Living Architecture.* Tr. by K.M. Leake. New York, 1964.

Engel, Carl. *The Music of The Most Ancient Nations.* London, 1929.

Erman, Adolf. *Life in Ancient Egypt.* New York, 1971.

Field, J.V. *Kepler's Geometrical Cosmology.* London, 1988.

Gadalla, Moustafa. *Egyptian Cosmology: The Absolute Harmony.* USA, 1997.

Gadalla, Moustafa. *Egypt: A Practical Guide.* USA, 1998.

Gadalla, Moustafa. *Historical Deception: The Untold Story of Ancient Egypt - Second Edition.* USA, 1999.

Gadalla, Moustafa. *Pyramid Handbook.* USA, 2000.

Gadalla, Moustafa. *Exiled Egyptians: The Heart of Africa.* USA, 1999.

Gretz, Ronald J. *Music Language and Fundamentals.* USA, 1994.

Hambidge, Jay. *Dynamic Symmetry.* NYC, USA, 1920.

Hambidge, Jay. *Dynamic Symmetry in Composition.* Mass., USA, 1923.

Hickmann, Hans. Musikgeschichte in Bildern: Agypten. Leipzig, Germany, 1961.

Hickmann, Hans. *45 Siecles de Musique Dans L'Egypte Ancienne.* Paris, France, 1956.

Iversen, Erik. *The Myth of Egypt & Its Hieroglyphs.* Copenhagen, 1961.

James, T.G.H. *An Introduction to Ancient Egypt.* London, 1979.

Kastor, Joseph. *Wings of the Falcon, Life and Thought of Ancient Egypt.* USA, 1968.

Kepler, Johannes. *Epitome of Copernican Astronomy and Harmonies of the World.* Tr. by Charles Glenn Wallis. New York USA, 1995.

Kepler, Johannes. *The Harmony of the World.* Tr. by E. J. Aiton. USA, 1997.

Kepler, Johannes. *The Secret of the Universe.* Tr. by A.M. Duncan. New York, 1981.

Lambelet, Edouard. *Gods and Goddesses in Ancient Egypt.* Cairo, 1986.

Moessel, E. *Die Proportion in Antike und Mittellater.*

München, Germany, 1926.

Peet, T. Eric. *The Rhind Mathematical Papyrus*. London, 1923.

Pennick, Nigel. *Sacred Geometry*. New York, 1982.

Piankoff, Alexandre. *The Litany of Re*. NY, NY, 1964.

Plato. *The Collected Dialogues of Plato including the Letters*. Edited by Edith Hamilton & Huntington Cairns. New York, NY, USA, 1961.

Plutarch. *Plutarch's Moralia, Volume V*. Tr. by Frank Cole Babbitt. London, 1927.

Polin, Claire C. J. *Music of the Ancient Near East*. NY, 1954.

Sachs, Curt. *The Rise of Music in the Ancient World*. NY, 1943.

Sachs, Curt. *Rhythm and Tempo: A Study in Music History*. NY, 1953.

Siculus, Diodorus. *Vol 1*. Tr. by C.H. Oldfather. London.

Speaks, Charles E. *Introduction to Sound*. CA, USA, 1996.

Wilkinson, J. Gardner. *The Ancient Egyptians: Their Life and Customs*. London, 1988.

Wilkinson, Richard H. *Reading Egyptian Art*. NY, NY, 1994.

Several Internet Sources.

Numerous references in Arabic language.

Sources and Notes

I believe that a researcher should not be content with referring to a single (or a few) references to support a point. It is my belief that to search for the truth, several sources must be considered and evaluated, and pieces of evidence must be put together like pieces of a puzzle, in the right location and time. A single reference may (and often does) intentionally/unintentionally leave out something, or color it.

As a graduate civil engineer with over 30 years of experience, I am qualified to comment on matters related to mathematics, geometry, building materials, and construction techniques. Academic Egyptologists are basically archeologists whose views on technical issues are beyond their qualifications. They are basically qualified diggers, and not interpreters.

Almost all my sources are written by very biased authors, who (consciously or sub-consciously) have pro-Western and/or Judeo-Christian paradigms. The vast majority of these references are condescending or show a disdain for ancient Egyptians and their traditions.

Western academia has made Greece the cornerstone of their racist Western heritage. In the process, they lied and twisted the truth. They use the "scholarly" trick, i.e. make a fact based on another reference, which is based on another reference, ...etc. At the end of this wild goose chase, you find no supporting archeological evidence. For example, they gave credit to Pythagoras, even though there is not a single piece of evidence that came from him or his immediate students. They invented the term, *Pythagorians*, so as to have an open-ended way of infinitely piling up achievements to this vague "European" term.

Listed references in the previous section, Selected Bibliography are only referred to for the facts, events, and dates, not for their interpretations of such information.

The absence of several references in the Selected Bibliography does not mean that the author is unfamiliar with them. It only means that notwithstanding their popularity, they are worthless as credible sources, for factual information.

Knot 1

General - Badawy, Choisy, De Cenival, Moessel, Pennick.
Kepler - Kepler (*Harmony of the World*)
Mozart - Brophy
Mystery Plays - Plutarch, Gadalla (*Egyptian Cosmology*), Kastor
The Circle (as the archetype in ancient Egyptian works) - Moessel (pgs. 4-5, 14-16, 19, 21-33)
Egyptian cord - Badawy, Pennick
Ra - Piankoff

Knot 2

Ma-at - Gadalla (*Egyptian Cosmology*), Kastor, Plutarch
Music - Engel, Gretz, Plato, J.G. Wilkinson, Hickmann, Polin, Sachs
Graphic Representation of Sounds - Speaks
Frets and Villoteau - Engel (pgs 51-53)
Time-beating - Polin (pg 35)

Knot 3

Ra and Atum - Piankoff
Music and the circle - Field, Kepler (*all three references*)
The circle (as the archetype in ancient Egyptian works) -
    Moessel (pgs 4-5, 14-16, 19, 21-33)
Definition of the curve (of the roof by a system of coordi-
    nates) - DeCenival (pg 146)
Neb symbol - Gadalla (as measured in the perfectly executed
    hieroglyphs in the open-air museum of the Karnak
    Temple)
Ennead - Piankoff

Knot 4

Primary Sources:
    Tehuti - Gadalla (*Egyptian Cosmology*), Kastor
    Graphic representation of sound forms - Speaks
    Squaring the Circle - Peet, Chace
    Tehuti and Language - Plato, Gadalla (*Egyptian Cosmology*)

Secondary Sources:
    Erman, James, J.G. Wilkinson

Knot 5

Primary Sources:
    Numbers & Mathematics - Peet, Chase
    Neb (Golden) Proportion & Summation Series - Badawy
    Additive Rhythms of Egyptian Music - Sachs (*Rhythm &
        Tempo*, pgs 90-95)
    Number mysticism - Assmann, Gadalla (*Egyptian Cosmol-
        ogy*), Plutarch

Secondary Sources:
Numbers & mathematics in ancient Egypt - DeCenival,
Erman, James, J.G.Wilkinson
Neb (Golden) Proportion - Pennick

Knot 6

Primary Sources:
Ra - Piankoff, Gadalla (geometric analysis)
Two Parts - Peet, Chace
Pentagon and Five - Gadalla (*Egyptian Cosmology*),
Plutarch
Neheb-Kau - Kastor, Lambelet
Shu and Tefnut - Piankoff, Gadalla (*Egyptian Cosmology*)

Secondary Sources:
- Erman, James, J.G.Wilkinson

Knot 7

Primary Sources:
Spirals in Ancient Egypt - Badawy, Lambelet, Hambidge (*both
references*)
Logarithm and Spirals - Gadalla being an engineer
Root rectangles - Hambidge (both references)
Double Square - Badawy, Gadalla (*Pyramid Handbook*),
Hambidge (*both references*)
Heb-Sed - Gadalla (*Exiled Egyptians, Pyramid Handbook,
Historical Deception*)
Ptah - Gadalla (*Egyptian Cosmology, Exiled Egyptians*)
Tehuti and Heru - Gadalla (*Egyptian Cosmology*)
Neb (Golden) rectangle - Badawy, Hambidge (*both refer-
ences*)

Secondary Sources:
  - Erman, James, J.G.Wilkinson, Badawy

Knot 8

Primary Sources:
  - Badawy, Gadalla (*Egyptian Cosmology*), Plutarch, Pennick

Secondary Sources:
  - Erman, James, J.G.Wilkinson
  - Badawy, Gadalla, Plutarch, Choisy (pgs 52-55), Pennick
  - Gretz

Knot 9

Primary Sources:
  - Diodorus, Iversen, Gadalla (*Egyptian Cosmology*), Plutarch, Plato
  Geometric Analysis - Gadalla (being an engineer)

Secondary Sources:
  - R.Wilkinson

Knot 10

Primary Sources:
  - Badawy, Gadalla (*Egyptian Cosmology*)

Several books are written about this subject, but they are
unworthy of referring to by name. These books, while
talking about art, split hair over the measurements in
ancient Egypt's artistic representations. The paramount
factor in art is PROPORTION, and not measurements.
These academicians missed the forest for the tree. In
reality, they missed both. Measurements are not the
subject of this book.

Knot 11

Primary Sources:
  Written Specifications - Badawy
  Harmonic Design Principles - Choisy (pgs 50-57), Badawy,
    Moessel (pgs 4-5, 21-33)
  Design and Construction Plans - Badawy, DeCenival
  Roof Definition - Badawy, DeCenival

Secondary Sources:
  - Erman, James, J.G.Wilkinson

Knot 12

Primary Sources:
  Function/Objective of the Temple - DeCenival, Gadalla (*Egyp-
    tian Cosmology*)
  Walls - Badawy, DeCenival, Hambidge (1920 ed.)
  Wall Joints - Gadalla (regular visits and being a civil/struc-
    tural engineer)

Knot 13

Primary Sources:
  Analysis of Pre-Dynastic Mastabas - Moessel (pgs 21-22, 32)
  Giza Mastaba Tomb No. 6 - Reisner/Badawy

  Other tombs during Old Kingdom - Moessel (pgs 22-23)
  Khufu's Granite Room - Badawy
  Pyramid Temple of Khafra - Badawy
  Menkaura Pyramid - Gadalla (*Pyramid Handbook*), Badawy

  Peripteral Chapel of Sen-usert I at Karnak - Badawy/Lacan and Chevrier, 1946 (verified by Gadalla on location)
  Wahka Tomb - Badawy/Steckeweh, 1936

  Karnak Temple - Badawy/Chevrier, 1936, Gadalla (*Egypt: A Practical Guide*)
  Ausar (Osiris) Temple at Abtu - Badawy/Calverley, 1933 (verified by Gadalla on location)
  Tomb of Ramses IV - Pennick

  Nectanebo II Temples - Badawy/Ricke, 1960

  Miscellaneous items - Moessel (pgs 30-31)
  Applications of Canon to Everything - Moessel (pgs 30-31)
  Capitals of columns - Badawy/Borchardt (1897/Hölscher, Morgan)
  Stelae - Badawy/Lange & Schäfer (1902, Hölscher)
  Pylons & Doorways - Badawy/Hölscher, Moessel (pgs 25-26), (verified by Gadalla on location)

Secondary Sources:
  - Erman, James, J.G.Wilkinson

Index

Heb-Sed, 77, 167
Heliopolis, *see* **Onnu**
heptagon, 91 ; and the **Neb** (Golden) triangle, 91
Hermopolis, *see* **Khmunu**
Hermetica, 10
Herodotus, 10
Heru, and the 3:4:5 triangle, 22, 52, 88-9 ; and Ennead, 41, 82 ; and musical rhythm, 35-6 ; and **Tehuti**, 80-1 ; as symbol of air, 21 ; definition, 167
Het-Heru, and music, 35 ; and temple of Dendara, 112 ; definition, 167
hieroglyphs, and application of harmonic laws, 48 ; Chairemon on, 95 ; Clement of Alexandria on, 95-6 ; Diodorus on, 95 ; geometric shapes of, 96-9 ; Plato on, 94 ; Plotinus on, 96 ; Plutarch on, 94-5 ; symbolism of, 92-9 ; sound and form of, 47
Horus, *see* **Heru**

I

Isis, *see* **Auset**

J

Josephus, Flavious, *see* Flavious Josephus

K

Karnak temples, ancient Egyptian name of, 54; columns at, 158-9 ; gateways at, 164-5 ; Pavilion of **Sen-Usert** I at, 144-5 ; pylons at, 98-9, 148-9, 162-3 ;
Kepler, 16-7, 173 ; and ancient Egypt as his sole source, 16-17 ; and the circle, 16-7, 39-40 ; and musical proportion, 42-4, references on/by, 173
Khafra, pyramid (erroneously known as *mortuary*) Temple of, 58, 116, 140-1
Khmunu, 49, 50, 67
Khufu Pyramid's granite room, 118, 138-9

L

Leiden Papyrus, and number mysticism, 41, 53-4, 82
Luxor, Temple of, 115 ; sanctuary (Holy of Holies) of, 49

M

Ma-at, as cosmic order, 25 ; as the law of creation, 25, 38 ; and harmony (music), 25, 26 ; and musical rhythm, 35-6 ; and Ptah, 79 ; glyph, 57

72-83 ; root 5 rectangle, 78-9
Rhind "Mathematical" Papyrus, 52-3, 62-4
Roman era, temple restoration during, 112, 156
roofs, definition of curve of, 40, 119

S

Sachs, Curt, 29,
sacred geometry, 169 ; *also see* Harmonic Proportion
Saqqara, Pyramid Complex, *see* Zoser
sarcophagus of Ramesses IV, 152-3
Sed Festival, *see* Heb-Sed
Senmut (archt), 111-12
Sen-usert I, pavilion of, 144-5
serpent, and spiral form, 67 ; and creation, 67 ; and duality, 67 ; as symbol for universe delineation, 38
Seshat, as Enumerator, 51 ; her cosmic activities, 51 ; *see details of her related activities throughout text*
Sesostris I, *see* Sen-usert I
Set, as symbol of fire, 21, 22
Seth, *see* Set
Seti I, pharaoh ; and temple of Abtu (Abydos), 150-1
Shabaka Stele, 80-1
Shu, 25, 68, 69, 86
significant points, 116
sound frequencies ; and form, 46 ; *see also* music

spirals, and creation, 67 ; and hieroglyphs, 67 ; and musical harmony, 84 ; and Neb (Golden) Proportion, 83 ; and Ra, 84 ; and Summation Series, 82-3
square, 49, 72-5 ; double-square, 76-7, 118, 138-9, 157
squaring the circle, 49, 53, 72 ; and the Grand Ennead, 49 ; and the Perfect Tone, 49 ; and Ra, 49 ; and Tehuti, 49
stanza, meaning of, 15, 171 ; of Leiden Papyrus, 53-4

star, five-pointed, and number symbolism, 71
stelae, definition, 169 ; sample harmonic analysis of, 160-1
Summation Series, 57-61 ; and art , 60-61 ; and Egyptian musical rhythm, 58-9 ; and human figuration, 60-1, 104 ; and musical terms, 59; and the Neb (Golden) Proportion, 60 ; and temples/tombs design, 116-7

T

Ta-Apet, 37, 54, 73, 111, 144, 148, 152, 158, 162, 164 ; *also under* Karnak temples *and* Luxor Temple
Tefnut, 25, 68, 69, 86
Tehuti, 26, 27, 169 ; and the Ennead, 49 ; and the equilateral triangle, 66, 87 ; and Heru, 80-1, 127 ; and the octave, 50 ; and squaring the circle,

Tehuti Research Foundation

Tehuti Research Foundation (T.R.F.) is a non-profit, international organization, dedicated to ancient Egyptian studies. Our books are engaging, factual, well researched, practical, interesting, and appealing to the general public. The books listed below are authored by T.R.F. chairman, Moustafa Gadalla.

Visit our website at:
http://www.egypt-tehuti.org
E-mail address: info@egypt-tehuti.org

About Our Books

Pyramid Handbook - Second Edition
ISBN: 0-9652509-4-6 (pbk.), 192 pages, US$11.95

A complete handbook about the pyramids of ancient Egypt during the Pyramid Age. It contains: the locations and dimensions of interiors and exteriors of the pyramids; the history and builders of the pyramids; theories of construction; theories on their purpose and function, the sacred geometry that was incorporated into the design of the pyramids; and much, much more.

Historical Deception
The Untold Story of Ancient Egypt - Second Edition
ISBN: 0-9652509-2-X (pbk.), 352 pages, US$19.95

This book reveals the ingrained prejudices against ancient Egypt, from both the religious groups, who deny that Egypt is the source of their creed; and Western rationalists, who deny the existence of science and philosophy prior to the Greeks. The book contains 46 chapters, with many interesting topics, such as the Egyptian medical knowledge about determining the sex of the unborn, and much, much more.

Exiled Egyptians: The Heart of Africa
ISBN: 0-9652509-6-2 (pbk.), 352 pages, US$19.95

Read about the forgotten ancient Egyptians, who fled the foreign invasions and religious oppressions, to rebuild the ancient Egyptian model system in Africa, when Egypt itself became an Arab colony. Find out how a thousand years of Islamic jihads have fragmented and dispersed the African continent into endless misery and chaos. Discover the true causes and dynamics of the history of African slavery. Understand the genius of the ancient Egyptian/African religious, social, economical, and political systems.

Egyptian Cosmology: The Absolute Harmony
ISBN: 0-9652509-1-1 (pbk.), 160 pages, US$9.95

Discover the remarkably advanced Egyptian cosmology, which continues to be the Ancient Future of mankind and the universe. It is the ONLY metaphysics of all (ancient and modern) that is coherent, comprehensive, consistent, logical, analytical, and rational. This book is informative and well written, so that the whole spectrum of readers, from the casual to the serious, will find the subjects enlightening. The book surveys the applicability of Egyptian concepts to our modern understanding of the nature of the universe, creation, science, and philosophy, such as the Big Bang, and their enduring cosmic consciousness that All is One and One is All.

Tut-Ankh-Amen: The Living Image of the Lord
ISBN: 0-9652509-9-7 (pbk.), 144 pages, US$9.50

This book provides the overwhelming evidence from ar-
cheology, the Dead Sea Scrolls, the Talmud, and the Bible
itself, that Tut-Ankh-Amen was the historical character of
Jesus. The book examines the details of Tut's birth, life, death,
resurrection, family roots, religion, teachings, etc., which
were duplicated in the biblical account of Jesus. The book
also reveals the world's greatest conspiracy and cover-up,
which re-created the character of Jesus, living in another
time (Roman era) and another place (Palestine/Israel).

Egypt: A Practical Guide
ISBN: 0-9652509-3-0 (pbk.), 256 pages, US$8.50

Experience Egypt! From the lively Nile Valley, to the
solitary deserts, to the diverse Sinai, to the lush oases, to the
exotic underwater life of the Red Sea, to the Mediterranean
beaches. A no-nonsense, no-clutter, practical guide to Egypt,
written by an Egyptian-American Egyptologist. Quick, easy,
and comprehensive reference to sites of antiquities and rec-
reation. Find your way with numerous maps and illustrations. Tips are included to help understanding both the modern and ancient Egyptian cultures. This pocket-sized book
is informative, detailed, and contains an illustrated glossary.

Tehuti Research Foundation

Ordering Information

Name_____

Address_____

City_____

State/Province_____   _____

Country _____Tel. (____) _____

_____ Books @ $11.95 (Egyptian Harmony)   = $

_____ Books @ $19.95 (Historical Deception)   = $

_____ Books @ $11.95 (Pyramid Handbook)   = $

_____ Books @ $ 9.50 (Tut-Ankh-Amen)   = $

_____ Books @ $ 9.95 (Egyptian Cosmology)   = $

_____ Books @ $ 8.50 (Egypt: Practical Guide)   = $

_____ Books @ $19.95 (Exiled Egyptians)   = $_____

Subtotal = $

North Carolina residents, add 6 % Sales Tax   = $

Shipping: (N. America only) $2.00 for 1ˢᵗ book   = $

for each additional book $1 x _____   = $

Outside N. Amer. (per weight/destination)   = $_____

Total = $

Payment: [ ] Check (payable: Tehuti Research Foundation)
      [ ] Visa [ ] MasterCard [ ] Discover

Card Number: _____

Name on Card: _____ Exp. Date: ___/___

Tehuti Research Foundation
P.O. Box 39406
Greensboro, NC   27438-9406   U.S.A.
Call TOLL FREE (North America) and order now 888-826-7021
Or FAX your order   212-656-1460
e-mail: info@egypt-tehuti.org